S0-CMQ-000

Understanding
Church Finances

Understanding Church Finances

THE ECONOMICS OF THE LOCAL CHURCH

LOYDE H. HARTLEY

THE PILGRIM PRESS
New York

Copyright © 1984 The Pilgrim Press
All rights reserved

No part of this publication may be reproduced, stored in a retrieval system,
or transmitted in any form or by any means, electronic, mechanical, photo-
copying, recording, or otherwise (brief quotations used in magazines or
newspaper reviews excepted), without prior permission of the publisher.

Library of Congress Cataloging in Publication Data

Hartley, Loyde H., 1940–
Understanding church finances.

Bibliography: p. 265
1. Church finance. I. Title.
BV770.H29   1984   254.8   83-23769
ISBN 0-8298-0708-X (pbk.)

The Pilgrim Press, 132 West 31 Street, New York, NY 10001

CONTENTS

vi

LIST OF DIAGRAMS, TABLES, AND CHARTS

PREFACE

Economic problems make a common denominator among otherwise widely differing religious groups. While this book describes the economic conditions in mainline Protestant denominations, the conclusions and recommendations put forward would have been impossible without the cooperation of local churches with orientations variously characterized as ecumenical or cultic, orthodox or radical, ecclesial or neoevangelical, fundamentalist or humanist. The Grace Brethren Church, the Church of Scientology, the United Methodist Church, and denominations of whatever distinctive stripe all have similar economic realities to face. Illustrations in this book depict these widely diverse groups on one hand to show the common threads of concern about how to finance religion, but on the other hand to note some innovative approaches to church finance emerging among some of the newer religious groups. While religious groups may disagree theologically and morally, there may be ways they can learn financial strategies from one another that do not compromise theology and morality.

The lay leaders of congregations who gave hours of time

telling stories, providing illustrations, and sifting through decade-old records made this book possible. They have shared more than financial information. They have shared visions of their congregations' present and future ministry.

This research was supported by a grant from the Lilly Endowment, Inc. to Hartford Seminary's Center for Social and Religious Research. The Lilly Endowment's interest in and concern for the financial well-being of congregations has encouraged a series of inquiries about economic aspects of church life by Hartford Seminary.

The whole project has been greatly aided by Elizabeth Nordbeck, David Roozen, Claude Dencler, Francis Ringer, George Schreckengost, Marjorie Hall Davis, Peggy Fennell, Helen Mummaw, and LouAnn Ernst. In addition to those who helped with writing cases or with analysis of data, Jackson W. Carroll, director of Hartford Seminary's Center for Social and Religious Research, has provided overall supervision and wise counsel for this project. Deep appreciation is also expressed to Kathy D. Jansen of Hartford Seminary for typing the final draft. The book is dedicated to my wife, Carol, in the hope that the congregations we love may prosper in their ministries.

Understanding
Church Finances

INTRODUCTION

On the surface, the American Protestant congregation appears to be a simple economic entity. Its members give money to pay the preacher, support good causes, and keep the building in repair. Beneath the surface, the financial operations of every congregation prove to be more complex. Many church leaders charged with their congregations' financial well-being find this complexity confusing and disheartening. As a result, they have limited insight into how financial health can be achieved by their congregations.

Local church finances have their own peculiarities. Business and family finances sometimes serve local church leaders as convenient but inaccurate analogies for their congregations' finances. Churches, unlike families, obtain most of their income from gifts and invested funds. The congregation's market basket—the goods and services it must purchase—includes salaries, enormous utility bills, benevolences to denomination, and sometimes large expenses for music. None of these are characteristic of families. Moreover, churches do not pay taxes. Local church finances are also unlike business finances, in that the church does not sell a product, does not have inventories, and does not count profits and losses as businesses do. Conventional wisdom about church finances derived from family or business finances, therefore, proves inadequate for the leader seeking financial health for a congregation.

Offerings, benevolence payments, denominational subsidies, cemetery funds, mission programs, building funds, contributions to police and fire departments in lieu of taxes, hunger relief drives, every-member solicitations, volunteered time and expertise, gifts in kind: these and other aspects of the congregation's financial life combine to make the local church unique among money-handling institutions. On one hand, this unusual mix of financial operations appears to have helped many congregations survive in environments where businesses, industries, schools, clubs, and community services have failed. On the other hand, financial failure characteristically leads to the closing of churches.

This book demonstrates how a relatively simple systems model of a congregation's financial transactions can be helpful in explaining economic aspects of church life and in identifying strategies that can lead to financial health. Defined as the ability of a congregation to acquire the necessary resources to accomplish its intended ministries, financial health is distinguished from mere financial growth. What strategies lead to financial health? Does this mean obtaining more income or introducing economizing measures or changing priorities? How can financial growth and decline be anticipated? How can church finances be managed more effectively? What do church leaders need to know about the financial life of their congregations? What is the theological importance of church finance? What national economic trends have impact on local church financial problems? What can be done to increase income and cut expenses without reducing the church's effectiveness? These questions have guided the analysis of the financial operations of the 75 congregations providing historical financial data for the research reported in this book.

4

Drawn from mainline Protestant denominations, these local churches provided information that may be used for comparisons with similar local churches. Several additional churches with especially typical or merely unusual economic circumstances are cited as illustrations throughout the book. These illustrations come from such theologically diverse and socially varied groups as the Seventh-Day Adventist Church, the Metropolitan Community Church, and independent fundamentalist groups. Even among the 75 mainline congregations there is diversity of size, community type, and goals for ministry.

Chapter I presents in summary the recommendations resulting from the inquiry. Readers may wish to return to this chapter after reading the entire book. The recommendations, while informed by both the comparative and illustrative data reported in subsequent chapters, are not limited to conclusions directly and narrowly drawn from the data. In some instances, the recommendations simply encourage good planning procedures, based on the general finding that many congregations do little or no financial planning.

Chapter II explores approaches to a theology of church finance in contradistinction to a theology of stewardship. While concepts of stewardship are deemed valuable and necessary, they provide an insufficient basis for explaining the theological importance of church finances. To remedy this shortcoming, a theology of the purposes of the local church is introduced.

Chapter III reviews the general economic climate of the nation and of national denominations. Implications for local churches are identified for trends in giving to religion, inflation and recession, unemployment, tax laws, membership increase and decline, employment of women, population shifts, and changes in the amount of money people have to spend.

Chapter IV presents a systems model of the flow of money through the church and of decisions related to the flow. This model guides the research reported in following chapters, but it also has value in helping local church leaders to locate financial problems in their congregations and to select among many available strategies for addressing those problems.

Chapters V and VI report the major research results of the study of 75 congregations' financial operations, along with a description of the methodologies used. Chapter VII recounts the opinions of local church financial leaders about their jobs.

Chapter VIII provides some tools that may be used in planning a church's financial operations.

The major part of the Appendixes is made up of case studies of six churches, which may be used as teaching exercises for local church leaders. Study and discussion of the cases will help leaders analyze the financial problems of the churches and identify ways of resolving them. Exploring these financial problems, even though they may be vastly different from the situations faced by the leaders' own congregations, will sharpen the perception and analytical skills of the people responsible for resolving the financial problems in their own churches.

CHAPTER I

Some Elements of a
Financial Strategy
for the 1980s

This chapter provides a summary of the basic results of an inquiry about local church finances. The summary is in the form of recommendations that local church financial leaders may consider for adoption. The following chapters provide elaboration and illustration of the recommendations in this chapter, as well as a framework or model for showing how the various parts of the local church's economic life are inter-related.

Economic conditions that precipitated fiscal problems for many churches in the 1970s and early 1980s, according to most predictions, will be even more severe throughout this decade. Utilities and maintenance costs continue to skyrocket, notwithstanding the general recession, and the accumulated effects of the past decade's inflation are only beginning to be understood. As a result, many congregations are facing more serious economic decline than their pastors and lay leaders admit. If these local churches emerge from the present decade with their present ministries and missions intact, fiscal planning must now become a priority, especially in churches that have done no such planning. Should the nation experience a major economic turnaround, planning will be no less a priority if the ministries and missions of local churches are to be effective.

Some local churches do, of course, withstand decades of economic adversity and still survive in some form or other. Such is the case of the congregation called LUCK, described in Appendix I. Many denominational officials have been mistaken in predicting that particular congregations will disband. The weakest of congregations may be a better risk, from an actuarial point of view, than the healthiest of church leaders. But mere survival is not enough. Each congregation has its own spirit, its own particular mission and ministry, which can be irretrievably altered when denied adequate financial support, even though some form of organizational life continues. This chapter presents, therefore, only a series of tentative conclusions, ideas, and suggestions. Because the congregations studied are but a small sampling of Protestant congregations in the United States and because the financial environment in which congregations seek to survive and grow is itself unpredictably changeful, these conclusions are best left tentative.

Many people willingly give advice to local church financial decision makers, much of which is based on limited experience. The advice givers are fund raisers, writers of denominational guidebooks, denominational staff people, bankers, and professional financial consultants. Some materials written by these people are included in the bibliography. Their advice has to do mostly with how to raise funds through obtaining regular contributions, but may also deal with budget con-

8

struction, theology of giving, motivation for giving, and even, to a limited extent, money management techniques. Fortunately, much of the advice is good. Some churches are growing financially, and even most of those in economic decline can forestall closing their doors.

The financial strategies proposed in this chapter do not consist of advice that churches are asked to adopt in blind faith. No single plan will work for everyone. To the extent that advice is given at all, it is to urge congregational leaders to plan all parts of the church's finances as an integrated system—not just a budget and an annual solicitation for contributions. Congregations, it will be shown, are more complicated financial systems than budgets and financial campaigns. Perhaps local church financial operations will need to become even more elaborate than they presently are in order to maintain healthy local churches. Therefore, while no single congregation will use all the ideas listed below, every congregation with 50 to 2,000 members and $10,000 to $1,000,000 in its annual budget should find at least some ideas that can be helpfully applied to its situation.

The first step in developing a sound fiscal strategy is to identify the results in ministry desired by the congregation—that is, what the congregation is seeking to accomplish. Goals need to be understood both theologically and in terms of the practical demands they place on the congregation. Each goal requires certain resources for its accomplishment—time, materials, expertise—all of which need to be identified. Then, after setting goals and listing the required resources, an appropriate process needs to be set in motion for acquiring the income to purchase resources and to transform them into the desired results. The results are then used or consumed, and members make periodic evaluations to insure that the results remain the desired ones, that resources are adequate and appropriate, that income is sufficient, and that the process as a whole continues to be effective. That, in summary, is the framework for local church financial planning advocated in

9

this book. By understanding local church finances as a system, the financial decision makers can better decide which directions to follow, which advice to heed. This approach above all is a theological affirmation of the local church's purpose tempered by the history, context, and membership of the church.

All the specific recommendations in this chapter assume that local church financial operations can be understood as a system: income such as money and volunteer time is transformed by processes such as budgets and programs and worship services into resources to produce desired results called ministries, which are used in the context of the local church itself and its community. Therefore, the chapter is divided into five parts, with recommendations about income, results, resources, consumption and evaluation, and economic and social environments.

Income: Where Will We Get the Time and Money?

Many local church financial difficulties can be reduced to income problems. Costs are fixed or going up, and buying power is going down because income has not kept pace with inflation. Demand for volunteers to do the work of the church is up, but because of population decline or changes in the work force the number of volunteers and the time they have to give are down. Principal causes of income problems include declining numbers of people making contributions of time and money, reductions in the average amounts of time and money being contributed, and inflation. All three can cut deeply into the reservoir of income every local church needs to produce and maintain its ministry. In the chapters that follow, a variety of secondary factors can be seen as contributing to each of these causes. For further elaboration of the sources of local church income, see Chapter VI.

For example, there may be fewer persons contributing because an ethnic change has occurred in the community surrounding the church, causing people to transfer membership elsewhere. Unresolved conflict and anger may reduce the amounts of time and money the congregation can expect to receive. (See Leas and Kittlaus' book *Church Fights*.) In other congregations, the death or retirement of the major contributor or the fact that several members are unemployed leads to reduced size of contributions. Elsewhere, contributions of time and money may be reduced because persons managing the church's finances seem to place little emphasis on soliciting contributions. All the above examples point to problems of income—not enough time, money, or expertise to do what the church needs to do in order to be faithful.

Moreover, the traditional answer to problems of income— get more people to give more—seems to work in fewer and fewer situations. What can be done, then, when income shrinks?

Because of the strong dependency of almost all local congregations on the regularly contributed gifts of active members, churches that have little opportunity for growth in membership often fail to explore other sources of income. For example, there are local churches that receive major support from wills and bequests, rental of property, interest from endowments, auctions of contributed goods and services, bazaars, fairs, and private enterprises. Others receive major income from sister congregations or from denominational funds because of the importance of their particular ministries. A few Protestant churches even sponsor bingo games. Among the 75 congregations analyzed herein, the average church received only 18 percent of its cash income in 1979 from sources other than the offering, up from 14 percent in 1970. A few received all their income from offerings, and, in contrast, one church received 67 percent of its income from nonoffering sources. Many churches facing income shortages, it seems clear, have not adequately explored increasing their nonoffering income. Several suggestions for doing this follow. When any of these nontraditional sources of income is pursued, special care needs to be taken not to lose the regular income from member contributions. People may think their individual contributions are no longer needed. Care also needs to be taken not to compromise the church's mission simply for the sake of getting more money. Income serves results, not the other way around.

Money from novel sources of income notwithstanding, increases in offerings and regular giving are the most frequently reported reasons for long-term improvements in churches' income, especially in congregations with growing memberships. Persons providing data for this study repeatedly emphasized their opinion that when members understand the need, they willingly give. See, for example, the interpretative budget of Otterbein Church in Appendix I. This opinion is supported further by the fact that per-member contributions often increase in churches whose survival is threatened, presumably because the remaining members have a clear understanding of the need for their contributions. The potential income from offerings may be much more than is presently realized in almost every Protestant congregation. One Seventh-Day Adventist congregation participating in this study reports a per-member annual contribution of slightly over $1,000, roughly 8.3 times that of the other churches studied. At the other extreme among persons interviewed for this study, there were wealthy lay people who paid the minimum required to remain members in good standing, in one case only 25 cents per year. And in another case there were those who actually sold their blood to raise funds for their fledgling denomination. In the Church of Scientology, as in several other religious groups, adherents pay large designated contributions as they advance in that group's hierarchy of training programs. The point is that members do contribute when they are convinced their congregation's life and ministry is vitally important and know their contributions make it possible. Protestant churches that do little to help lay people understand the significance of their gifts miss a most important aspect of their caring ministry to their contributors as well as the opportunity to increase income. Successful television preachers do not make this mistake.

The use of any new income-producing plan needs careful scrutiny before it is undertaken, as noted above. Almost all such efforts attempt to translate volunteer time of laity into cash. For example, let us suppose that a congregation needing more money to pay its pastor's salary and its heating costs decides to sponsor a church fair complete with carnival rides for children, booths, and food stands. Being good planners, almost all the members are involved in preparations for a month before the actual fair and a few leaders for much longer than that. The fair is successful, raising $15,000. Let us further suppose that a month after the fair seven new church-school teachers need to be recruited, but they are unavailable because capable people feel their time is already overcommitted to the church. The keys to deciding whether to undertake an income-producing project lie in determining realistic answers to four questions. How much income will result? Does the project contribute in ways other than financial to the ministry of the church? How much time will it take, and how would that time be used if the project were not undertaken? Will the project energize participants or drain their energy?

Among congregations with large numbers of older members, the most likely source of income in addition to regular contributions is through wills and bequests solicited through a deferred-giving program. Although most denominations have produced materials explaining how to start deferred-giving programs, only a very few congregations actually solicit funds in this way. Among the 75 congregations included in the study, only 29 percent report having a deferred-giving program. Only three of the 75 churches report having programs that were more than marginally successful. Perhaps this is because financial leaders in local churches, while knowing how to solicit weekly contributions, have not learned how to help support the church through obtaining personal wills and

13

bequests. Yet many people with moderate or small estates do contribute in this way when the opportunity is available to them. A church implementing a deferred-giving program needs to make prominent announcements of the program several times throughout the year and to continue such announcements indefinitely. Moreover, the church needs to be prepared with expert advice to help people write or rewrite their wills. This is in and of itself a ministry, because it helps people to confront their own finitude and to discover responsible stewardship of their life's accumulation of goods and money. In some instances, large churches or even a cooperative group of smaller churches may choose to implement annuity programs that guarantee lifetime income to persons making bequests. People do not have to wait for their death to make major contributions that do not threaten their financial security. Educational institutions and other charities have had success in such ventures. While income from bequests and wills represents the source of income second only to regular offerings in local churches, it requires much work and a long time before any results are seen. Some wills produce their income a half century or longer after they are written. Obviously, short-term cash problems cannot be mitigated using this strategy, but it remains the best way to establish the long-term fiscal solvency of a congregation.

In some instances, congregations can manage their investments so as to produce more income. There is certainly nothing sacred about placing funds at 5¼ percent in accounts insured by the federal government. There are many safe investments that produce better returns and are equally liquid. Even certificates of deposit, bank money-market funds, and U.S. Treasury notes, all of which have the backing of the federal government, can be purchased so as to mature at one or two-month intervals, meeting the congregation's need for liquidity and interest. One church in the sample of 75 provides a typical illustration. Its endowment of approximately $250,000 earned annual income of $12,500 in its passbook savings account. Every year this interest was used to pay for building maintenance. In a 9 percent certificate of deposit, the income would have been $22,500, and had the church invested in money-market funds in the late 1970s and early 1980s, it might have earned as much as $37,500 or more annually. It is possible to make more venturesome investments of church funds without jeopardizing their safety. For example, churches and educational institutions have increased the growth of their endowments with very little risk by purchasing stocks and selling options to buy the stocks they own. In this way a sizable percentage of gain is almost always possible. The amount of money churches have, often in small accounts for such things as cemetery endowments, building funds, organ replacement funds, and women's groups' bank accounts, is surprising, and it might be better used to serve the church's ministry. Leaving such funds in passbook accounts at local banks may mean they suffer greatly from the ravages of inflation. Of course, investment strategies must change with the times. Today's safe investment may be tomorrow's loss. No simple answer to the local church's investment policy will work forever. The rationale "We've always done it this way" is especially inappropriate in this aspect of church finance.

If no increase in the amounts or kinds of income required can be obtained, the only alternative is to redefine goals so they realistically match expected income. In short, expenses must be cut, which is what the next section of this chapter is about.

Results: What Must We Do to Be Faithful?

Every church uses its income to bring about some kind of desired result. The result may be clearly articulated and plain for all to see. It may be vague or jumbled in a mass of personal expectations of individual members. Nevertheless, every congregation uses its money to accomplish something. This "something" is here called results. Results may be understood as the major goals of a congregation and as the means to achieve these goals. The major goals point to the theologically important results of the congregation. These vary dramatically from congregation to congregation. For some, the major goal is found in service in Christ's name to people who suffer in any way. For others, it is nudging the world, nation, and neighborhood toward justice and peace. Other congregations find their major goal in proclaiming God's word to non-Christians. Still others seek to provide members and others a place to escape their worldly problems and to contemplate the eternal God. The goal may be simply that members believe God is rightly worshiped. Of course, a congregation may have any or all these goals, plus several others.

The means used to accomplish these major goals are even more varied, and themselves represent intermediate results: having a comfortable, warm building for worship and service; paying money to mission programs; teaching members and their children; employing a pastor; conducting worship; promoting protests; talking with people about commitment to Christ; sponsoring fellowship programs; counseling distressed persons; offering the sacraments and rites of baptism, holy communion, marriage, burial of the dead, and confession of sin and assurance of pardon. All these reflect the church's desired results.

A local church's budget, if it is a reasonably accurate prediction of how the money will actually be spent, is a remarkable reflection of the desired results of the congregation. At least it says where the money goes, if not how the contributed energies and abilities of the members are used. Changes in how congregations spend money for resources usually means there have been changes in desired results, which in turn means changes in the goals of the congregations.

Some congregations have financial problems particularly related to the result side of the economic system. The building is too expensive to heat, too many people are employed by the church given its income, major maintenance can no longer be postponed. The problem is that the existing desired results can no longer be offered given the church's income, or that the results require more money to achieve than they have in the past, perhaps even major capital investment. The strategies listed below all have to do with modifying the results expected by the congregations. Often such changes can be accomplished without serious negative effects on the basic purposes of the congregations. For further elaboration of the results sought by congregations, see Chapter II.

With a little historical research, church leaders can identify the specific impact inflation has on specific desired results of the local church. The leadership of some sample churches seems to have deluded itself by taking comfort in small increases in actual income received each year and ignoring the annual decline in purchasing power due to inflation. From 1970 to 1980, for example, income would have had to increase by more than 100 percent just to keep up with inflation. Each congregation, by monitoring the particular effect inflation has had on the amounts spent for particular goods and services regularly purchased, can determine whether or not the piecemeal decisions made over a span of years have actually served to undercut the real goals of the congregation, as is apparently too often the case. This can be done by constructing charts like those in Chapter VI, Charts 6 through 14, which portray changes in how church funds are spent over a period of years.

If the budget does not reflect the congregation's true priorities, cuts can more easily be made in nonessential areas of expenses. Leaders can be intentional about what savings the congregation wishes to effect. Among congregations contributing data for this volume, the proportion of dollars spent for pastoral services has been going down; for utilities, up; for benevolences—after a sharp downward trend in the 1970s— slightly up. According to the opinions of church leaders, funds for pastoral services are least likely to be cut, but, in fact, they have not kept up with inflation and in some instances have been cut severely. By more clearly identifying the areas in which they wish to economize, congregations may more easily set strategies to realize savings.

Many churches could study the short- and long-term economic strategies devised by other congregations to determine their applicability to their own situation. Economizing measures often have little or no detectable effect on the desired program while effecting large savings in, say, utilities and maintenance costs. Congregations have implemented such measures as retrofitting buildings with more efficient heating and cooling units, sharing buildings with one or more other congregations, changing to a more economical heating fuel, changing the location of winter meetings to a home, buying heating fuel and other commodities in cooperation with several congregations to obtain lower prices, installing larger containers for fuel to enable bulk purchase, and installing multienergy-source heating and cooling equipment to allow shifts from one fuel to another. In some instances, congregations report that reducing the temperature in the building has required them to end leasing of offices or meeting rooms during the week. Others that formerly contributed space to community service organizations are now less willing to do so. These changes must be counted as liabilities against the savings realized by lowering temperatures. Some congregations did major renovations and replacement of equipment earlier than was absolutely necessary because they correctly anticipated the effect of inflation on building costs.

Not all economizing measures relate to the building and its maintenance. Some congregations have cooperated with others in joint purchasing of choir music. In one instance, a church with a 9:00 A.M. worship service jointly purchased altar flowers with a neighboring church with an 11:00 A.M. service. New congregations and congregations without facilities, of course, can make enormous savings by sharing buildings with other congregations, as in the case study of one of the churches reported in Appendix I.

Often it becomes necessary to consider with care substitutions for market-basket items that have become too costly for the church. As inflation increases, certain resources formerly purchased by the church become too expensive. When this occurs, skill to assess the relative equivalency of the substituted resource is needed. For example, will the nonprofessional youth director be as effective as the professional one? Will the reduced funds of the church music program reduce the quality of music? How much can the music quality be reduced before it negatively affects the total worship? Can lay people be trained to do on a volunteer basis some of the things the pastoral staff does now? These are very subjective and very difficult questions, but they need to be answered if leaders intend to make substitutions responsibly.

Some churches need to consider alternative staffing models. Some congregations are purchasing specialized pastoral services by the day. In this way those congregations that cannot afford a full-time minister of education, for example, can get some expert help in areas such as curriculum development, teacher training, and youth work. The same approach might be used for nonprofessional staff. The 1980s may well be the decade for the rapid growth of lay ministry, with lay people developing the competencies to perform many of the tasks previously undertaken by professional staff.

Denominational leaders need to articulate more clearly the benefits of services rendered to the congregation or on its behalf by the denomination in relation to dollars contributed by the congregation. According to the survey reported below, benevolences for denominational use would be among the first items to go should the congregation be faced with financial crisis. The low priority given the denomination may reflect the low value members place on these services. Communication needs to be strengthened between the denomination and local leadership about how the funds spent by the denomination accomplish the results desired by the local church.

Some costs for local churches go up or down according to the number of members; others do not. Member-related costs include such items as costs for church publications, church-school materials, food for fellowship programs, and, if it is based on membership size, the contribution paid to the denomination. Nonmember-related costs do not change with the size of the membership. If there is an increase in the number of members, the cost per member goes down; if membership decreases, the cost per member goes up, sometimes dangerously. Table 9 in Chapter VI reports this kind of data for the sample of churches studied. Mortgage payments, utility bills, and salaries are usually nonmember related.

Distinguishing between member-related and nonmember-related costs is important for four reasons. First, adding member-related costs to the budget will be somewhat self-correcting if there is a decline in membership, and therefore somewhat safer assuming the item is affordable in the first place. Second, the larger the proportion of member-related costs, the better able a congregation is to handle a decline in members, because costs collapse as the number of members go down. Third, making this distinction can show how much a congregation can grow before major new costs must be added (e.g., sanctuary enlarged, additional staff employed). And fourth, some congregations, especially new church starts or congregations in extreme financial distress, may be able advantageously to treat as member-related costs items that are nonmember-related in most congregations. For example, if a new congregation is renting space for worship from another congregation, the rental payment may be based on the size of membership rather than a flat fee. Or a church seeking a part-time pastor may pay a salary based on the number of people attending.

If adequate resources cannot be secured and if cost-cutting

will undercut the purposes of the congregation, major changes in the results are inevitable. The foregoing strategies regarding the production of results assume changes can be made without fundamental alteration in the church's main goals for its ministry. When this more severe situation occurs, however, changes in the church's purpose and goals become acutely necessary. Some examples make this point clearly.

One congregation that has a strong sense of community service operates a food pantry out of their inner-city church building. For many years they were able to help anyone who could establish a legitimate need that could not be met by some other agency or service. Because of cuts in denominational funding and because people have become less willing to contribute staples to the pantry, the desired result—meeting every legitimate need—could no longer be met. After an extensive search, no new funds or food could be found. The church decided to give groceries to a particular family only once every five months, and then only when it was facing acute emergency. The result is different, but the church's overall goal in ministry is still being addressed.

Other congregations make similar economically necessitated modifications in their expected results when they drop children's church-school classes because volunteer leadership cannot be found, or cut the pastor's travel allowance, or no longer pay for soloists and section leaders in the choir, or drop from two full-time clergy to one aided by a part-time retired person. These are net losses in the church's program. Cutting church program in these ways, even when it is absolutely necessary, is dangerous, according to the financial leaders in many congregations, because the support of people who were highly committed to these ministries may be lost. "We can't cut the soloists," one pastor pointed out, "because one of them is the church's largest contributor." When such cuts are necessary, people who are most involved in the area being cut need to be convinced of the necessity of the decision and to help find ways to obtain similar results. Moreover, at times

21

the church will have to live with the painful consequences of hard decisions.

Acquisition of Resources: How Does Income Become Translated into Results?

In a sense all church programs, personnel, and property can be understood as processes in the life of the congregation. All these help the church accomplish its mission goals. The processes discussed here, however, are limited to those that have direct economic applications to the work of the local church financial leader—in short, financial management. For further information about the acquisition of resources, see Chapters IV and VII.

In most congregations, budget preparation is the single most important financial process undertaken. As the key plan for purchasing the resources necessary to accomplish the church's desired results, it requires more time and is more widely discussed among members than any other aspect of church finances. Yet many church budgets seem arcane to the rank and file of members. Budgets need to be documents that interpret the congregation's objectives in terms of specific necessities. Comparison of the sample budgets from two congregations in Appendix II demonstrates this concern. The first church, which owns rental properties, is in a state of acute fiscal crisis. One of its major renters is moving out, resulting in the projected income falling far short. The second has experienced a 50 percent loss of members over the past 15 years, yet its income has actually held constant; its income for 1982 was 9 percent over 1970. Each budget reflects the spirit of its congregation. The budget of the former is a budget sheet, showing projected losses and gains over the previous year. The budget of the latter is a narrative, detailing how objectives were translated into finances. The latter church has not only been successful in subscribing its budget, but has done so solely from contributions of members. Chapter VIII explains further the value of interpretive budgets.

Church leaders need to seek help in managing endowments and small bequests of from $10,000 to $500,000. They need more insight into what interest from endowments can and cannot do. One pastor, for example, complained, "I'm not sure what goes on with our little endowment fund. The bank sends us checks every year, but no one at the church knows how much is in the endowment or what restrictions are placed on it." Another congregation completely lost track of a bequest of $12,000, which a former pastor had set up in their behalf. These situations are not atypical. Because the bequests are relatively infrequent, expertise in handling them is negligible. Moreover, even leaders who have expertise in business finance are on unfamiliar ground with wills, bequests, trusts, and endowments. Moreover, because the endowments are comparatively small, churches cannot afford to pay for much expert advice. But there are several financial objectives that can be set for such funds, depending on the needs of the congregation: capital gains; income; security; and flexibility, so that the income from endowments and bequests can be used for objectives that change from time to time. The management of these funds begins by encouraging the individuals who make major gifts and bequests to do so in a way that allows the church to benefit maximally from their generosity. Usually, this means the fewer restrictions the giver places on the use of the gift the better. Moreover, the regular contributors need better interpretation of the bequests lest they assume their own regular gifts are no longer necessary. Endowments are difficult for church leaders to discuss openly, and often seem to be shrouded in misunderstanding by laity and clergy alike. A more frank and open analysis of their potential and limits would lead to healthier management. A caution: the church that becomes dependent on income from its endowment for fixed necessary costs may have to close if the endowment does not produce the necessary income. Moreover, endowment funds are especially vulnerable to inflation, as indicated by the poor performance of many endowment funds during the past decade. Bankers, who sometimes are sought out by churches to invest their endowment funds, often have limited understanding of the congregation's financial need. This, of course, is not their fault; churches have not described what their need actually is.

Assuming no congregation wants to invest in high-risk securities, two basic decisions need to be made. Will the investment be made for purposes of maximizing capital growth or income? Will the church need to have all or a large part of the cash available on short notice (liquidity)? Most congregations invest their endowment to produce high-interest income—for example, certificates of deposit—when in fact they might be better advised to invest in capital growth. Some financial consultants for educational-institution endowments say growth is the only appropriate objective. If income is needed by a church that has invested for growth, some of the principal is sold, perhaps on a basis not exceeding 6 percent of the endowment's principal per year or 50 percent of any year's growth. In monitoring endowments, leaders need to be able at least once a year to report the market value of the holdings, how much of the growth has occurred because of new funds added to the endowment, and how much of the growth is the result of the efforts of management.

The 1980s will see congregations use technological advances as they become available and affordable. Because churches produce services for people, technology has not significantly increased production in the past. In fact, the last significant contributions made by technology to churches may be the microphone and the copying machine. During the 1980s, microcomputer software is being developed that will allow pastoral care of church members to be accomplished more thoroughly and efficiently; for example, computers can keep track of bereavement anniversaries. The special skills people are willing to contribute in kind can be recorded and recalled as the need arrives—the plumber who is willing to fix a leaky faucet, for example. And church financial records can be kept to help identify important trends, so that some modeling of alternative financial futures can begin to take place.

For many congregations, however, the most important management innovation to introduce is normal, accepted accounting procedures, such as books set up in a consistent pattern, a regular audit by disinterested persons, and bonding for treasurers and others who handle money. Person after person interviewed for this study reports receiving the books of the church in piecemeal fashion. Some churches lose track of their assets, or have only canceled checks to show how their money has been spent. Others have so many different accounts—each church-school class and each society or fellowship group having its own—that it is impossible to tell what assets the church really has.

Fortunately, almost all people who handle church money are honest, even if ill advised about how to give account of their work. One congregation studied for this report was not so lucky. The church had a trusted treasurer who grew up in the congregation. Year after year he gave reports of the value of the endowment and the income it produced. Later all of this was proven fictitious. He had in fact embezzled all the church's endowment and borrowed unauthorized thousands of dollars in the church's name. He was not bonded, so the church lost an amount it cannot even estimate accurately, but in excess of $30,000. Sobered by this turn of events, the church obtained the volunteer services of an able financial consultant, a member of another congregation who was looking for a way to use his competence in the service of the church. The consultant concluded, after several months' study, that the loss by embezzlement was not the church's most serious financial problem. More serious was the fact that the church leaders had no idea of where funds would be coming from week to week in order to carry out the church's ministry. Payrolls might not be met, taxes for nonordained employees were not being withheld and sent to the government, deferred maintenance loomed threateningly. Although this congregation had initially agreed to be one of the 75 presenting data for this study, its subsequent discovery of the embezzlement and the general poor condition of its records precluded its participation. Chapter V describes in more detail the poor record-keeping and financial management in some congregations: no budgets, no posting of expenses, no balancing of checking accounts.

Churches that go through economic decline may go through a series of identifiable thresholds rather than proceeding on a straight, gradual downward trend. They may slip gradually downward to a threshold, dive sharply through it, then slowly decline to the next threshold. What is lost by passing through a threshold may be very hard to regain. As a result, financial planners need to be alert to these thresholds. They differ from congregation to congregation, but the following thresholds are most frequently mentioned by pastors of the economically declining churches. They depict a plausible though not necessary sequence.

1. Attendance and membership decline.
2. Offerings have a declining rate of increase.
3. Total offerings decline, although individual members contribute more.
4. Nonprofessional staff is dropped and not replaced.
5. Quality of music suffers and paid staff is let go.
6. Major maintenance is postponed.
7. Church depends on gifts, bequests, and endowments for operating costs.
8. Adult education and fellowship is curtailed or abandoned.
9. Church uses bequests and principal from endowment for annual expenses.
10. Professional staff is reduced in size.
11. Professional staff is reduced to only one part-time minister.

12. Children's education and fellowship is curtailed or abandoned.
13. Emergency maintenance causes financial crisis.
14. Churches merge.

When these things happen, particularly if they happen rapidly, the members describe their feelings in terms not unlike those used by people experiencing grief: anger, denial, bargaining, depression, and eventually expressed resigned acceptance. The feeling level in the congregation has an impact on pastoral ministry and on people's desire to give.

Consumption and Evaluation: Who Benefits from the Church's Ministry?

While a local church's ministry is usually not thought of as a product, it is nevertheless produced with considerable effort. People benefit from their use of what the church produces to build their faith, to fulfill their call to serve others, to learn, to experience awe, to experience the aesthetic, to worship God. Accordingly, some recommendations about the constituencies that use the church's results can be made.

Financial leaders need to be aware of the growth or decline in the constituency for each result desired by the congregation. For example, one large downtown congregation offered to the public a classical Christmas concert every year. From 1950 through 1975, the concert packed the sanctuary, but since that time there has been steady decline. Preliminary inquiries indicated that older people, the principal constituents of the concert, were fewer in number in the area surrounding the church and more reluctant to leave home at night. Awareness of changes like these in the constituency for particular ministries can alert financial planners to changes in the circumstances or needs of constituencies that are forthcoming and thereby provide important lead time for decision making. Moreover, as in the case of the church with no youth and no prospect of attracting youth that nevertheless wanted a

27

youth minister, awareness of the constituency can help decision makers avoid serious mistakes.

To what extent, if any, are the constituents of any particular ministry expected to provide income to support that ministry? In some instances particular ministries might be dropped if the people for whom the ministry was conceived do not support it financially. For many other ministries, such as youth ministries or food and clothing distributions, little financial support is expected from the constituents. When one group pays for a ministry and another group is the principal beneficiary, both groups evaluate the ministry. Both sets of evaluations need to be taken into account in financial planning.

Evaluation of the financial affairs of a congregation is closely related to evaluation of the church's program of ministry, but separable from it. The audit is the usual way of evaluating the church's finances. It asks if the money has been spent as it was supposed to have been, and thereby establishes the financial integrity of the church and its leaders. Although periodic audits are necessary, they are not by themselves sufficient for the evaluation of financial operations. Below are listed five additional important evaluative questions not customarily addressed by the audit.

1. How many more constituents could each result have without increasing the cost? For example, how many more members could the church have before a new or expanded building would be needed or new pastoral staff added?
2. How much money can be spent for resources before each additional increment begins to produce diminishing results? For example, at what point does more money spent for educational materials or altar flowers or janitorial supplies cease helping people learn more or making the sanctuary more beautiful or getting the church cleaner?
3. Is the church spending its money for resources that will accomplish its goals? One definition of economics is that it is the science of distributing scarce resources among unlimited

goals. Clearly this definition applies to the local church, which invariably has many more opportunities for ministry than it has income and resources to address. Each expense, then, needs to be evaluated against other ways the same money could be spent, given the opportunities the local church has.

4. What competition does the church have in offering particular ministries? Are other churches or service agencies doing the same things? Given the scarcity of income and resources, most congregations cannot afford to compete with other congregations in offering, for example, the same kind of food-pantry service to poor people when no one offers help with housing or legal services.

5. To what extent, if any, do members require the maintenance of particular ministries for their total support? One pastor of a congregation studied for this report said his New York City congregation paid $65,000 per year for the music program. If that much were not spent, and the music quality were to decline, members would leave and the whole financial stability of the church would be upset.

These five questions reflect the need for congregations to seek evaluative information beyond what is usually provided in the audit, or for that matter in the budget. They require a more holistic picture of church finances than is currently available to most church leaders. Such a holistic picture is possible only when the church's financial decisions are made in the context of the church's social environment or its demographic niche.

Economic and Social Environment: A Demographic Niche

Church financial decisions occur in the context of an environment much larger than the church itself. Leaders in inner-city churches are acutely aware of how the communities where they are located have affected their congregations. But the importance of the community's impact is just as great for suburban congregations, even if it is less obvious. The social and economic environment in which a local church engages in economic activity is called in this book a demographic niche. The word *demographic* is chosen because of the importance of the number and kind of people living in the area surrounding the church and their level of income for predicting whether a church has the opportunity to grow economically.

Leaders need to monitor the reasons why people join the church or leave the church's membership. Basically, people join a church in only two ways: by transfer of membership from another church or by baptism and confirmation. Incoming transfer members differ according to whether their transfer was occasioned by a change of residence. People who join a church for the first time may be children of existing members, children of nonmembers, or adult converts. People who leave church membership exit by one of three channels: death, transfer, or removal by action of the church. Diagram 1 depicts the flow of persons in and out of membership of a local church.

Financial planners need to know the dynamics of the flow. For example, is the number of persons transferring from churches outside the area increasing or decreasing? What is it about the church that attracts (or repels) these persons? Is the number of persons moving into the community increasing or declining? What is the number of persons leaving membership by transfer to other area churches? What are the reasons for their departure? Is the loss avoidable? What happens to people who are removed from the church rolls because of inactivity? What is the result, if any, of efforts to reinvolve them in the life of the church? Mainline Protestant churches have traditionally grown largely by the baptism and confirmation of members' children and by transfers from other churches outside the community. As the average age of members in mainline congregations increases and the number of children declines, less growth resulting from baptism of

DIAGRAM 1

Sources of Membership Growth and Decline

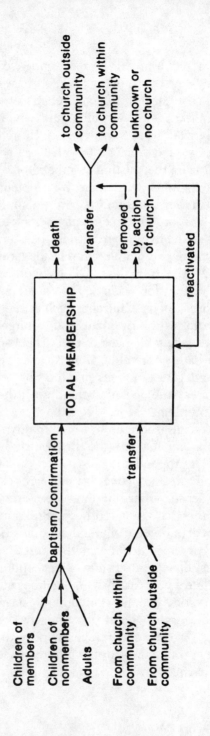

members' children will be realized. As communities change ethnically or decline in population, fewer transfers will be available. In the future, congregations will need to attract more of their members from adults who have not previously been baptized, from transfers from churches within the same community, and from groups that are socially or ethnically different from the existing membership.

Some churches face economic problems because of major changes in their communities. For example, one community's economy is largely dependent on a large army installation, which is slated to move from a northeastern to a southwestern state. One of the sample churches is located in this community and expects to lose half its membership immediately when the transfer occurs. The long-range implications are even more serious. Churches such as these need the support of judicatories to evaluate and redirect their objectives. Churches facing changes of this proportion with large debts are especially vulnerable. Congregations newly started in the past two decades in areas that did not develop into the residential areas anticipated at the time of the church's start face similar problems. More often, however, the church in economic decline is located in a community that is itself in long, slow economic decline (see the case study "St. John's of Metropolis" in Appendix I).

Most Protestant congregations are parishes in the geographic sense. Their buildings were erected to serve people in the immediate neighborhood. Preliminary investigation of the growth or decline of members in relationship to the population growth or decline in the postal zip code where the congregation is located shows an exceptionally strong association. While a great many congregations attract members from distant points, people who commute many miles to worship are often people who at one time lived close to the church building. Protestant churches appear to have difficulty attracting new members from more than a few miles away. As a result, changes in the community's population have direct bearing on the number of members and financial well-being in the parish church.

In contrast to the parish church and its strong ties to the community stands the cathedral-type church. The cathedral attracts its financial support from afar and is not as vulnerable to community changes. While most Protestant churches are parishes, there are examples of cathedrals. The National Cathedral (Episcopal) in Washington raises money throughout the world for its building fund and ministry. Similarly, the Crystal Cathedral of TV preacher Robert Schuller receives funding from diverse quarters alerted by the mass media. The Assemblies of God, a rapidly growing conservative Protestant group, has started urban regional congregations that are successful in attracting people from great distances. These congregations usually have large church-bus fleets and make effective use of regional media, but they are not especially closely tied to the immediate surrounding neighborhood. In fact, the site for this kind of congregation may be selected because of easy access to urban transportation arteries or because of location in an upper-middle- to upper-class neighborhood where members do not presently live but may aspire to live someday.

Churches in economic decline that appeal to a small socioeconomic or ethnic group are in particularly difficult situations. If they can attract persons of other age groups, economic standings or ethnic backgrounds, their chances of survival are much greater. A heterogeneous church is not dependent for its survival on the continued support of any particular homogeneous group. Often, ethnic churches want to grow by attracting people like themselves or by reactivating former members. Rarely can this be done when the church is already experiencing decline. This observation, and the recommendation for churches to move toward heterogeneity of membership that derives from it, runs counter to much church-growth theory published in recent years. The church-growth theorists, such as Wendell Belew,

George Hunter, Donald McGavran, and C. Peter Wagner, recommend building homogeneous memberships. They contend that a single kind of people—with similar if not identical values, interests, and personal characteristics—should be recruited into membership of a church that wants to grow. In addition to the theological objections that the whole people of God cannot be so arbitrarily divided and that local churches should reflect the diversity within the whole people of God, the idea that most established churches can grow by attracting more people like the present members simply does not work in churches like those studied in this volume. It is simply a demographic impossibility. Compare, for example, the case studies "St. John's of Metropolis" and "A Church Named LUCK" in Appendix I. St. John's died because it would not accept new members unlike existing members, and LUCK survived only because it did diversify. In many instances, a heterogeneous congregation can provide a kind of hybrid vigor in pursuit of the desired results or objectives of the congregation.

Summary

This chapter has listed some of the financial strategies currently being used or considered for use by local churches. Not all strategies will apply to every congregation, but most congregations can find one or more that will be helpful to them. The questions that follow can serve as a checklist to help church leaders review the kinds of information they need in making informed financial decisions. The same questions are helpful in analyzing the illustrative cases provided in Appendix I.

- What are the church's principal sources of income? How much income comes from contributions? What portion comes from other sources? What is the reliability of these other sources?

- What new strategies for increasing income might work?
- To what extent can giving through wills and bequests be promoted successfully?
- What objectives does the church have for income from investments? How is the endowment to be managed?
- What results is the church seeking? What are its goals? What ministries does it provide?
- Can the same results be obtained if some funding is cut?
- Can substitution of resources be made with the same results obtainable?
- What benefits does the local church get from its denomination?
- What costs in the church are related to the number of members? What costs are fixed no matter how many members the church has?
- Does the budget reflect the results the church actually wants? Does it accurately predict how the money is spent?
- Is the church facing important turning points or thresholds?
- Does the church follow some accepted process of record keeping?
- Is the church's potential constituency growing or declining? What changes are occurring in the neighborhood immediately around the church?
- What impact, if any, is the congregation making in the community?
- Who cares whether this church accomplishes its ministries?

In seeking to answer these questions, local church leaders will confront a common legacy which hinders effective financial planning. The elements of this legacy bind together the 359,797 various congregations in the United States and Canada, notwithstanding their diverse theologies and faiths. If the financial needs of these congregations are to be met in timely ways and with minimal trauma, the following elements of the legacy will require attention by the financial leaders.

- Nebulousness of mission and purpose: While purity of motive and singlemindedness have never characterized American congregations (some try to be all things to all people), the real challenge to local leaders is that of defining missions and purposes and that of using these definitions to assess results.
- Sacredness of particular goals: Almost every congregation has aspects of its existence (particular groups, programs, or buildings) which in the minds of the members are immune from financial review. Trauma increases when these goals are threatened. Leaders are challenged to interpret these goals in light of the larger mission and purpose of the congregation and in light of fiscal realities.
- Independence of spirit: Often church finance leaders act in ignorance of decisions made by program leaders, and vice versa. Some leaders act with total autonomy. The day of the lone church treasurer whose word on money is law must give way to coordinated planning.
- Inaccuracy and inadequacy of financial record keeping.
- Lethargy of self-perpetuation: Preoccupation with survival results in lethargy, which deadens sensitivity to criticism and slows decision making, even decision making directly related to the congregation's survival. Leaders must begin now to address the suitability of programs for constituents, the implications of deferred maintenance, the changes in community demography, and the costs of retraining clergy and laity for new missions and purposes.
- Contradictions of desires for homogeneous and heterogeneous membership composition: While many congregations in theory are willing to accept new members who are different from the existing members, few have learned how to cope with the differences and to benefit from them. Discovering and developing unity in diversity challenges every congre-

gation located in a changing community. Congregations like to have new members, but want clones of the
old.
- Fear of economic decline: Congregations have not
learned how to deal with retrenchment. Too often they
resort to easy solutions—endowment tapping, across-
the-board budget cuts, deferred maintenance, staff reductions or salary cuts, reductions in benevolence
giving. Churches in economic decline are challenged
to search their souls in assessing their mission and
purpose, to evaluate each program and service, and to
plan any phase-out with care.

CHAPTER II

A Theological Perspective on the Church as Economic System

Are there theological assumptions lurking in the approach taken to local church finances in this volume? Perhaps in nascent form such assumptions do exist, and this chapter attempts in a preliminary way to declare them. After presenting a consideration of the adequacy of the idea of stewardship as a theological basis for church economies, the chapter moves to an alternative theological approach based on the local church's understanding of its mission.

The Idea of Stewardship

Since the early nineteenth century, when the notion of stewardship was invented, largely in response to deplorable mismanagement of charitable funds and to serious financial difficulties in local churches, stewardship has dominated most theological discussions of church finances. The systems approach to economic aspects of congregational life taken in this book requires a broader theological basis than has been offered by the idea of stewardship or than is warranted by the etymology of the word steward.

The word steward is used to translate the New Testament Greek word meaning household manager, *oikonomos*. The word economy derives from this same Greek root. The English word steward, undeniably a good translation of the Greek meaning, has over its history elevated its meaning from its humble beginnings. In early English, the first syllable was spelled *stig*, which meant sty, a pigpen, and by extension a farmyard. The second syllable straightforwardly means warden or caretaker. So the word steward was originally used to refer to caretakers of livestock, or the cleaners of pigsties. From these low beginnings, the steward eventually gained position in the household—in the kitchen, pantry, and wine cellar—eventually gaining considerable control. Stewards were caterers. By the time the great country houses were being built in sixteenth- and seventeenth-century England, the steward had become the manager of the estate and of the nobleman's financial affairs.

The idea of stewardship has become in contemporary church usage more than an analogy. Stewardship is interpreted as a calling, a basic role model for contemporary church members. There are several problems in using the idea of stewards and stewardship in this way. First, although stewards are used as analogies in the parables of Jesus and in Paul's letter to Corinth, the New Testament usage never goes beyond metaphor. Stewards are not of the same category as prophets, apostles, teachers, healers, workers of miracles, or speakers in tongues. Never are Jesus' followers admonished to be stewards, and only in passing are they encouraged to be *like* stewards. Stewards do have some laudable characteristics, to be sure, especially if they are found to be trustworthy, faithful, and loyal. But stewardship is not presented as a basic calling in the New Testament. Second, there is no compelling contemporary counterpart of the house manager or steward. In previous centuries, people knew what a steward did. Today if someone said he or she was a steward, no clear understanding of that person's line of work would be apparent—union shop steward? wine steward? steward on an airplane? The analogy has much less power today than in Jesus' day. A Christian convert, upon being told to be a steward, would reasonably respond, "How do I do that?" The analogy loses its power, therefore, because of the elaborate explanation needed.

Moreover, two theological objections to the exclusive use of stewardship as the key notion related to the economics of congregations may be raised. First, stewardship insufficiently takes into account church members' understanding of dominion and vocation—that is, their power and their calling to use that power in God's work on earth. Church members are more than caretakers of God's work, they are both obedient servants and partners in the work. Second, the active God of history cannot aptly be characterized as an absentee landlord who leaves the management of affairs to underlings called stewards. God is fully active, as is the dedicated church member, in bringing about justice and peace in a war-torn, suffering, and inequitable world.

If the stewardship analogy fails to suffice, perhaps the underlying meanings people intend when using the analogy will prove enlightening. There are basically three in the literature: the steward as contributor, the steward as consignee, and the steward as conserver.

In its narrowest application, the word *stewardship* means ways to get money contributed to the church—another name for putting dollars in the offering plate or a euphemism for tithing. People writing about stewardship from the nineteenth century onward have tried to dissuade their readers from using this limited and limiting perspective. It has, nevertheless, survived as a popular notion despite these efforts. The stewardship campaign in most congregations is an effort to raise money. Being a good steward means being a sacrificial contributor. Of the three uses of the stewardship analogy, this one is the most closely aligned with local church finances.

Two broader notions of stewardship have emerged. The first of these does not limit stewardship to money, but includes also the time and talents of the church member. Every Christian is given gifts by God and, as a consignee, is accountable to God for the appropriate use of all gifts. This idea, expanded as a kind of personal ethic for all of life based on stewardship, is expressed succinctly in William J. Keech's book *The Life I Owe*. Everything we are and all we possess, according to this understanding of stewardship, are God's gracious gifts consigned to us for use according to God's will. Time, money, talents, family, life work, and capabilities are individual trusts with which we have been charged and for which we are morally accountable. Promoters of this understanding of stewardship urge church members to ask themselves such questions as those of Dennis Savage in his book *One Life to Spend:* "How much of my time do I give in serving God? What talents, abilities, and skills do I have? To what extent am I using them as a good steward? How can I grow in my stewardship?"

The second broader notion of stewardship casts the steward in the role of conserver of God's whole world and all its resources. Stewardship is not simply a personal, individualistic accountability, but is the collective responsibility of all people. Seen in this way, stewardship is a bridge between religion and the secular economy. The steward as conserver is accountable for the senseless destruction of God's world and is called to protect it from the ravages of atomic bombs, chemical wastes, and general secular avarice. The steward as conserver becomes an advocate for the earth. As Julian Hartt

41

puts it, "Oysters, egrets, golden plovers, peregrine falcons, leopards, grizzlies: they cannot speak effectively for themselves. Yet they deserve to be represented before the bar of justice. They do not deserve to die because humans value their own comfort and appearance and love of sport (call it kill) far above the lives of relatively defenseless creatures." Glenn Stone's book *A New Ethic for a New Earth*, from which the above quotation is taken, appeared along with many others of like title during the 1970s; to name a few: *Toward Stewardship: An Interim Ethic of Poverty, Power, and Pollution; The Ethics of Enjoyment; Can Man Care for Earth?; Crisis in Eden;* and *What Do You Say to a Hungry World?*

These two elaborations on the early notion of stewardship are indeed welcome. Their use of the steward metaphor is reasonably successful, although they encounter the same problems as listed above. Moreover, they move away from theological reflection on local church economics, still a worthy subject for such reflection. What is the theological significance of the people of God going about gathering the resources necessary to do the work of God at a particular time and place? What is the theological significance of their actual attempts to do God's work? What is God's participation in these activities? These are the questions that need to be addressed in a theology of local church finances.

Christians as Co-creators

One approach to addressing these questions is to understand the congregation and individual members of it as being co-creators with God in God's continuing creative activity. To continue the alliteration with contributor, consignee, and conserver, perhaps concocter or contriver would be better than co-creator, and less lofty too. This point of view is consistent with the personal opinions of many people interviewed for this study. When they were asked if they thought people's beliefs had very much to do with what they gave or with how the congregation's finances were handled, most (87 percent) said they thought beliefs were important. But when asked what beliefs were important, very few mentioned anything reflective of tithing, or "time, talent, and treasure," or environmental ethics. What they did mention was commitment to specific programs of their local church. "These are the things," they say in effect, "we are doing for the glory of God." They affirm what their congregations are *doing*. And, as respondents repeatedly mentioned, people support with their money those activities deemed important to the life of their congregations and important to the results of their congregations' efforts to serve God. Their opinions are more nearly characterized by the phrase "We would be building" than by "We give thee but thine own." People see themselves, not simply as caretakers or household managers (the root meanings of steward), but in some sense as being co-creators with God, called to bring into reality God's future.

The idea that people do in fact have more power than is implied in the term steward is consistent with the growing awareness that humankind has the power to alter the world fundamentally and irrevocably for good or ill. We have the creative power to say "Let there be . . . " and to concoct something altogether new. But we have not always been able to say, after we have lived with our concoctions for a while, "It is good." Chemical pollution, nuclear contamination, and disappointments in the early promises of technology have led us to be wary of our creative powers, but at the same time have evoked in us awesome awareness of those powers. Mere stewards, keepers of a lord's property, have no such prerogatives.

A creed written by Stephen W. Burgess and James D. Righter in *Celebrations for Today* reflects the creative cooperation possible in God's service.

> We believe in God our creator,
> who creates the universe and our earth;
> who continues to care for us.

We believe in our Lord Jesus Christ,
   who redeemed creation and all people;
   who continues to live with us.
We believe in the Holy Spirit,
   who empowers renewal and ministry;
   who continues to work through us.
We believe that Scripture, tradition,
   experience and careful thinking
   form guidelines for a growing faith.
We believe that we are starting here,
   in loving ways and obedient service,
   work worth finishing in heaven.
We believe we are being saved
   by the grace of God.
   Shout "Hallelujah!" and "Amen!"*

This point of view, while worthy of consideration, is not without its pitfalls. Congregations certainly are not infallible interpreters of what God calls them to create, and the plain truth is that all the works started here are not "worth finishing in heaven." While congregations have not yet created anything as menacing as a missile with a nuclear warhead, many congregations have fostered racism and sexism by alienating ethnically different people and reinforcing practices that discriminate against women. Many of the "Christian schools" started by Protestant congregations, for example, were built solely to allow members to avoid integration of races and to undercut public education. Any congregation that sees its work as co-creative also needs a way to confess its sins.

The idea of men and women being co-creators with God may be particularly unacceptable to those who interpret sin, especially original sin, to be the ambition of humans to become like God. Likewise, it will be unacceptable to those who understand all human works to be so thoroughly corrupted by

*From *Celebrations for Today* by Stephen Burgess and James D. Righter. Copyright © 1977 by Abingdon. Used by permission.

sin as to be worthless at best and fundamentally destructive at worst. The idea of people being co-creators with God requires, notwithstanding human sinfulness, the assumption that people are capable of doing good and are worthy of the dominion of the earth given them by God. Persons involved in the financial aspects of a congregation appear to have accepted the assumption that their actions can and do create something good, although there is wide divergence on what constitutes good. Nevertheless, authority in matters of church finances is power to do good or evil. The theological task of each congregation, then, is to discover how God calls it to co-create.

Moreover, any theology (or ethics) of congregational finances needs to reject dominion as a ground for exploitation. Power to control the church finances is not license to do as one will. Walter Brueggemann, in his book *The Land,* observes that the Hebrews had the promised land so long as it was only promised. When they tried to possess and exploit it for their own purposes, they lost it. Congregations may be in an analogous position. At one extreme, the financial resources of a congregation may be controlled by the church leaders for purposes of exploitation (the most drastic form observed by the research team was embezzlement, but many noncriminal forms of exploitation of church funds also exist, such as manipulating funds to gain personal prestige and to monopolize information about church finances). At the other extreme, the financial resources may be seen as the mechanism by which the congregation participates in creating God's future. The reality, of course, falls somewhere between the extremes, as illustrated by the case material collected for this study and included in Appendix I.

The traditional popular imagery of stewardship that casts church members as mere caretakers and managers of God's static, stable creation needs to give way to a more dynamic imagery that stresses the creative involvement of church members in God's historic purposes. In fact, the steward anal-

45

ogy may already be abandoned by many lay people. In its place, the notion of co-creatorship seems to be emerging, although that terminology is not yet popular. If people are made in the image of the Maker, that perhaps explains why people are makers too. The finances of the local church afford the persons who deal with these funds an opportunity to fashion and form, to generate and give birth to a church and world more in accord with God's purposes. If these opinions have merit, the starting point for a theology of church finance is the doctrine of the church; and the starting point for the doctrine of the church is an understanding of how people are working with God to create and give in a particular time and place.

Diversity in Congregational Theologies

Congregational theologies—particularly understandings of goals or purposes or objectives, called throughout this book the congregation's desired results—differ from church to church in substance and in degree of clarity with which they are expressed by the membership. Recently, theologians and sociologists have studied how different churches take on identifiable characteristics according to their understanding of who they are and of what God calls them to do. In his book *A Church to Believe In*, the Roman Catholic scholar Avery Dulles identifies six such currently operating images of the church: the church as the body of Christ, the church as the people of God, the church as institution, the church as sacrament, the church as proclaimer of God's Word, and the church as community of disciples. From a Protestant perspective, David Roozen, Jackson Carroll, and William McKinney, in a forthcoming book on the varieties of religious presence, identify four understandings of churches regarding their main ministry and purpose: the church as activist, the church as servant, the church as evangelist, and the church as sanctuary. A church with desired results in the area of ethical activism not only has a different theological self-

46

understanding from a church with desired results in the area of providing sanctuary for its members from a threatening social environment, but also has different financial operations. A church that sees itself as activist, as does the New Ark Church in the case study in Appendix I, wants results in redressing injustices in its community and in the world at large, but has comparatively little interest in owning buildings and property. A sanctuary church that calls its members from the worldly to the sacred realm, such as St. John's Church, also in Appendix I, is very much interested in its building and in isolating the building from its surroundings. At St. John's, this isolation was accomplished by chain-link fences and opaque but translucent plastic coverings on all windows.

A particular church's desired results find expression in many ways. Architecture of church buildings is sometimes an indicator. The spirit of a congregation in a cathedral-like Gothic structure makes a statement about itself to all who see the exterior of the building. While the more Byzantine church buildings may have very plain exteriors, inside they create a sense of the ethereal. The former makes a bold evangelistic statement, the latter deals in internal mysteries. They achieve different results.

Because congregations have different desired results and different degrees of financial well-being, four distinctions may be drawn.

- An economically growing congregation is one in which income is increasing at a rate faster than the rate of inflation.
- A programmatically articulate congregation is one in which there is consensus among members about the results desired; the results may even be stated in writing.
- An economically healthy congregation is one in which there is sufficient income to purchase the resources necessary to produce its desired results. An eco-

47

nomically healthy congregation must be programmatically articulate in order to know what resources it needs to purchase.

- A theologically defended congregation is one in which the desired results are articulated and determined to be supported by what the members believe to be God's will for them. Not all churches that can describe their desired results can defend them in terms of their theological traditions.

According to these distinctions, a church may be economically healthy and theologically defendable even though it is not growing economically. For example, one small congregation in an Appalachian coal town has declined financially in the past 20 years. Yet it continues to serve and will in the future serve the spiritual needs of the retired and unemployed coal miners who have not moved away from that community. Its income is sufficient to support this result, hence it is economically healthy. The members can express their goals and support them with their understanding of both scripture and the traditions of their denomination. Hence it is theologically defendable.

The results a local church seeks reflect its values, and because of this require theological interpretation and legitimization. Each result needs to be tested against the best theological criteria the congregation can obtain. If the result serves only the narrow purposes of a few members rather than the church's genuine, tested understanding of God's call, then it is unworthy. Likewise, all parts of the church's financial operation need to be evaluated in light of the results the church has tested and wants to accomplish. Are the financial operations of the church set up so that the necessary resources are acquired for the church to be faithful to its calling? Do the financial operations themselves contribute directly to some of the congregation's desired results—for example, helping people use their money in ways consistent with their faith? Do members know how their contribution made possible the desired results? Can the congregation realize economies in accomplishing the desired results? In seeking answers to questions such as these, a congregation can discover the theological importance of what otherwise might appear to be mundane financial operations.

The interrelationship between theology and critical financial decisions is illustrated by a Massachusetts United Methodist Church. The congregation, located in an outer-urban neighborhood which is experiencing demographic changes, learned that repairing their large 56-year-old gothic building would require expenditures of almost one million dollars. The condition of the church tower, with some stones so precariously balanced that the sidewalk was roped off to protect pedestrians, symbolizes the general long-deferred interior and exterior maintenance. At first members were inclined to raise the one million dollars to fix the building, but assets in this amount were unavailable from the 399 members or denominational sources. Then they considered selling their building and disbanding or moving to another, possibly suburban, location. But no purchasers were found. Upon further reflection and through considering their particular call to mission and purpose, the congregation has elected to stay in its present community. Having voted to demolish (at a cost of $80,000) their gothic monument, they will either erect a new, energy-efficient building on the same site or, possibly, share a building with a nearby congregation. Although the plans for a new building are not yet drawn, the members want the building to serve the needs of their community. Throughout the decision-making process, the church members have sought a sense of purpose and mission in their faith. In the terms listed above, the congregation has become increasingly theologically articulate. Their decisions are being defended in this way. Their economic health will be confirmed when they can show their plans are financially feasible—that is to say, they have sufficient income to purchase the resources needed to carry on their ministry in their present location.

CHAPTER III

National Trends and
Local Church Economics

Economists divide the general economy into three large sectors: the private sector, which is made up of all profit-making economic activity; the public sector, which includes all aspects of the government's participation in the economy; and the voluntary sector, which comprises all philanthropic activity. Macroeconomics is the study of how the government's participation in the economy has an effect on the relative prosperity of the private sector, and vice versa. Also within the purview of macroeconomics is the study of the effects of the voluntary sector, although this area of inquiry is only minimally developed in the literature of economics. Religion, when its economic aspects are studied, is considered part of the third or voluntary sector. The principal concern of the first part of this chapter is to identify how some national trends in the private and public sectors can have effects on a local church's finances. The effects are principally those that produce changes in the amount of money, time, and skill people have to contribute to their congregations. The second part of the chapter describes some aspects of the economic well-being of mainline denominations and lists implications for local churches.

There are several economic characteristics that distinguish religion, in particular the Protestant churches, from other voluntary philanthropic organizations. These characteristics make the macroeconomics of religion different from the macroeconomics of the voluntary sector as a whole. The American people characteristically give large amounts of time and money to voluntary organizations, and religious organizations receive more in gifts of time and money than does any other philanthropic activity. Giving to religious causes exceeds $20 billion annually, plus the value of volunteer work, which is estimated to be equivalent in worth to the dollars contributed. Religious organizations are almost totally dependent on these voluntary contributions for their economic survival, unlike other nonprofit organizations and even more unlike the private and public sectors of the economy. Nonprofit organizations such as hospitals, symphony orchestras, and universities collect fees and make service charges, have substantial endowments, and may use government funds in addition to the voluntary gifts of individual benefactors. While religious organizations receive about 46 percent of all money *contributed* to private nonprofit organizations, they have only about 15 percent of the *total income* of these organizations. Therefore, anything that increases or decreases the amount of money people contribute has a stronger impact on the financial health of congregations than on that of other voluntary organizations. Any trend that increases or decreases the expenses of congregations, independent of the amount of contributions, will also have a sharp impact on the financial health of congregations.

Thus the financial health of local churches can in part be

attributed to the overall economic climate of the nation. When people have more disposable income, for example, churches receive larger offerings. Congregations, like other institutions, have either benefited or suffered from recent general economic trends depending on a great variety of factors, several of which are discussed in this chapter. Many of these factors are far beyond the control of local churches: the opening and closing of plants and businesses, spiraling cost increases, shifts in population, national and international economic policies. Every local church needs to be aware of how these factors affect its income and expenses, even though the church has little or no ability to change them. The effects of some of the factors can be mitigated, however, by the financial decisions made and strategies followed by local congregations.

Trends in the National Economy

While leaders of congregations can do very little about fluctuations in the local economy, much less the national economy, they can be aware of how changes in the economy make a difference in their own local churches. They can even anticipate the consequences of future changes. The local effects of national trends vary from congregation to congregation. In the northeastern states, churches in heavily industrialized cities such as Johnstown, Pennsylvania have had severe reductions made in 1983 church budgets because of the recession, unemployment, and population decline. At the same time, some churches in Houston, Texas are growing faster than their planners anticipated in their most optimistic projections. Even within the same community, economic changes do not necessarily have the same effects on every congregation. A plant's closing may decimate one congregation and barely be noticed in another. One congregation may grow rapidly as the population increases, another may stay approximately the same size. By anticipating the effects of major changes in the economy of the community and the nation on the life of their congregations, church leaders can plan ways to operate most effectively given their particular economic environment.

The objective in this chapter is to name some important regional and national economic trends and to list their implications for local churches.

Inflation. During the 1970s and early 1980s, inflation received more sustained national press attention than any other economic change, yet the effects of inflation are variable and not well understood by many local church leaders. The most commonly used indicator for inflation is the Consumer Price Index (CPI), which is based on the consumption patterns of a typical American family. In some ways, the CPI is a good indicator for use by local churches. A large part of every dollar received by the church pays for salaries and expenses—about 29.2 cents for pastors' salaries alone in 1979 in the sample churches. Since the families of pastors and other church employees may be assumed to be reasonably typical of average American families, the CPI might be used as a yardstick to evaluate church staff salaries over a period of years.

But the CPI may seriously underestimate the effects of inflation on other parts of the church's market basket. Two major items in the church's budget—utilities and payments to denominations—illustrate this difference. Utility expense in 1979 averaged 10.9 percent of the sample churches' expenses. Most families do not spend this much of their total budget for utilities. Churches with large, poorly insulated buildings heated by older, inefficient furnaces and supported by declining numbers of members have a much greater proportion of their income consumed by utilities. Inflation precipitated by increased fuel costs, therefore, is usually more serious for congregations than, for example, inflation precipitated by increased costs for housing or food. Inflation in housing and food costs are more of a problem for families. Similarly, inflation in construction costs has important consequences for local churches, especially if the leaders decide to defer major maintenance as a strategy for coping with inflation.

The CPI has nothing to correspond to the payments that churches make to denominations. Moreover, there is no standard way to compute the cost to a local church for belonging to a denomination or for estimating the value the congregation receives in return. Therefore, while the CPI can be used as a rough yardstick for computing the effects of inflation in the church's dollar, it must be done with caution and qualification. If churches keep up with inflation, it is because they receive more income, principally in larger offerings. Even if they keep up with inflation, the changing price of major items in the church's market basket has required significant changes over the past decade.

The 75 churches reporting data for this book were paying a smaller proportion of their annual income in 1979 for pastors' salaries, contributions to denominations, educational programs, and maintenance personnel than they paid in 1970. (See Chapter VI for charts.) They paid a greater proportion of 1979 income for utilities, secretarial assistance, insurance, maintenance supplies, and capital expenses than they did in 1970. These data indicate that many churches are coping with inflation by using one or more of the following strategies: keeping cost of pastoral services down (usually by reducing pastoral staff size and by giving raises less than the rate of inflation), cutting back on funds given to the denomination, curtailing programs, and either deferring maintenance or soliciting volunteer help for maintenance.

Church leaders need to discover the consequences of each of these inflation-fighting strategies for the desired results of the congregation. If the strategy chosen undercuts the accomplishment of the desired results, the loss in contributed income may be greater than the savings realized.

Recession and unemployment. In the early 1980s, concern

about recession and unemployment has grown while inflation has remained a serious problem. Recession and unemployment have added significantly to the local churches' economic difficulties. Because of the effects of recession and unemployment, the United Methodist Conference in Michigan asked all pastors to accept no increase in salary for 1983. This request reflects the Conference's struggle not only with the economic reality of reduced income, but also with the symbolic problem of clergy getting raises when many people have no jobs. Recession places local churches in a kind of double bind—the need for the church's desired results (especially pastoral care and meeting survival needs of the poor) increases in times of recession while funds to support these desired results decrease. Quite literally, many congregations have to decide between paying the electric bill or feeding more hungry people. A lay leader in one of the sample congregations, a business executive, was asked what he would recommend if the recession became acutely severe in his community. He suggested, "Hire a third minister, because people would experience much increased personal and domestic stress and need more pastoral care and counseling." Yet he conceded he had no idea how his congregation could afford the additional expense.

The connectional systems of the denominations may be an important relationship in helping local churches deal with the double bind of recession. Congregations might ask for short-term reductions in the amount of money they pay the denomination or request denominational subsidies to underwrite ministries designed to reduce the hardship of recession. In some instances, congregations in communities not as severely affected by the recession have provided support for congregations where recession is severe. These are, of course, short-term strategies for coping with acutely severe recession in specific states or regions. A general, long-term recession would necessitate even more of a major change in local church finances, perhaps requiring that many presently underused and expensive-to-maintain church buildings be closed.

Tax laws. Changes in tax laws can make important differences in a local church's financial picture. At present, churches have two major tax advantages: the charitable deduction contributors receive for federal income tax purposes and exemption from paying most if not all taxes on property used for religious purposes. Property tax laws vary from state to state, and several state legislatures are considering changes in tax laws. If many churches were required to pay property tax at the normal millage rate for the municipality or county, the increased expense would have major impact on the churches' expense budgets, and would likely necessitate the disbanding of some congregations. A few congregations, acknowledging their indebtedness for police and fire protection, have made voluntary contributions to municipalities for these services.

The case for church tax advantages is made by Dean Kelley in his book *Why Churches Should Not Pay Taxes*.

Population shifts. For most congregations, shifts in the population are of more importance economically than either inflation or recession. Since local church income is closely tied to members' contributions, the number of potential members a congregation has can make the difference between a prospering and a struggling church. The United Methodist Church in Anguilla, Mississippi is typical of many congregations in this regard. During the 1970s, the population surrounding the congregation declined about 10 percent. Very few people have moved into the area, and those already there have traditional affiliations with other churches. If this congregation is to attract new members, it must compete with the other area congregations for decreasing numbers of new residents or attract members from existing churches, some of which are struggling and may be closing in the next few years.

The case study of St. John's Church (Appendix I) is another story of a church threatened by population shift. The ethnic group that founded St. John's increasingly moved to distant suburbs, and new ethnic groups moving into the area were not welcomed into the church. Where the population shift in a community involves an ethnic change, church leaders need to decide on a strategy of gradual integration of new ethnic groups into the life of the church or on a strategy of serving the original ethnic group until the ministry can no longer be financed. Most Protestant denominational officials urge the former strategy, but many congregations, like St. John's, follow the latter with the result that the church building is finally sold to a church serving the new ethnic group.

Churches in rapidly growing areas can expand with the population if such growth is desired. In growing communities, churches that do not increase their membership may be failing to attract new people for fairly obvious reasons or may be actually rejecting the newcomers. New residents may not be attracted to a church because it offers less than a total church program, because the members are involved in conflicts that are unimportant to new people, or because no one has identified what expectations the new people have of the church. In some instances, new members may be seen as a threat to entrenched leadership. Thus while population growth in the community served by a local church may produce increased numbers of members and as a result financial growth, such growth is by no means automatic. It requires the church to modify its desired results to take into account the needs of new people.

Volunteer time. In recent years, there have been major changes in the amount of time people have to volunteer to the church and in the expectations people have of the organizations where they volunteer. Encroachment on the amount of time people potentially have to volunteer has been made as the result of more women being employed in the work force, the number of persons holding two jobs, and the variety of leisure-time activities economically within the reach of most church members.

Because of the voluntary nature of Protestantism, symbolized by the offering plate as well as the volunteer church leader, changes in how and when people volunteer have far-reaching importance for the local church. With less time available to be volunteered, lay people may expect to maximize their effectiveness in the time they do have to give. Moreover, there is greater demand for training related to the volunteer activity. CONTACT Teleministries, an ecumenical telephone ministry serving most major American cities, is staffed by volunteers who have had a minimum of 50 hours of training and who periodically update their skills. Without such training, volunteer time cannot be accepted. CONTACT trains 2,500 to 3,000 volunteers every year. A number of theological seminaries are introducing or expanding lay education programs, some of which lead to graduate degrees in religious studies. In the future, if a local church wants people to volunteer, it may need to provide them with training that will maximize their effectiveness and personal satisfaction.

Summary. National trends need not surprise or overwhelm local churches. Church leaders can usually adjust their financial strategies to cope with the effects of such trends, unless they are caught unaware. Gradual changes in the national economy will require congregations to adapt, but will threaten the existence of only a few. Inflation in utility costs may reduce the number of days a church building is open during cold months, and inflation in salaries may require reduction in the pastoral staff and more reliance on nonprofessionally trained employees or volunteers. Nevertheless, congregations are showing they can and do make these changes without fundamentally altering their character or mission. The same desired results are sought; the resources used in producing them change.

Sudden changes, as opposed to more gradual trends, could be more life-threatening to congregations. For example, if they were required to pay property taxes, local churches with high property values would probably be forced to relocate or make major reductions in their programs. Churches in the centers of cities with large buildings and small congregations would be especially vulnerable.

Trends in Mainline Protestant Denominations

Information about general economic trends in Protestant churches sheds light on the particular problems faced by local church financial decision makers, although many local churches experience more serious economic difficulty than the general trends indicate. Conversely, some local congregations have enjoyed economic success during the 1970s notwithstanding the overall static, if not gloomy, picture. One United Methodist Church in Texas increased from only 8 charter members to more than 1,200 members in the years 1978–82. A United Church of Christ in Detroit closed because the membership had dwindled to 16 persons. Thus, not all churches are as well off or as poorly financed as the national trend indicates. While trends never tell the whole story, four basic conclusions about the economic condition of Protestant churches may be drawn from the annual statistical data reported during the past decade by the denominations themselves. The conclusions are:

- During the decade 1970–79 there was practically no real advance in the amount of money available to Protestant churches. Their buying power has remained constant.
- The number of clergy serving in these denominations has increased over this decade, potentially significantly increasing costs to local churches.

- The total membership of these denominations has declined (with some exceptions, noted below), reducing the number of contributors.
- There has also been a decline in the number of local congregations in denominations with falling membership.

Each of these trends is examined in some detail below.

The data gathered support these general conclusions. Projected over the next decade, these trends, if continued, bode serious financial problems for many individual Protestant congregations. The conclusion that Protestantism as a whole faces economic demise, however, is premature and unwarranted. Decline does not, in voluntary institutional terms, mean death. Local churches have been able, for example, to service major long-term decline by cutting expenses, or perhaps more accurately, by spending only what income they have in any particular year. While these trends, if continued, will mean major cuts in denominational programming, they will not mean the end of the denominations or the end of the economic importance of denominations.

Constant or falling real dollar receipts. People contribute more money to religion than to any other philanthropic cause. The American Association of Fund-Raising Councils, which monitors giving for all causes, estimates between 41 and 48 percent of all gifts were made to religion during each of the years of the past decade. In 1979, religious causes received 46.5 percent of all giving, a total of $20.14 billion. Chart 1 shows the total amount of giving to religious causes for the 1970s. While the amount given has increased from $8.30 billion to $20.14 billion, the deflated value of the contributions has increased from $7.14 billion to $9.21 billion. The shaded portion of the graph shows constant values of the dollar, deflating the value of the dollars contributed by using the Consumer Price Index. A local church's offering in 1979 would have to be 2.43 times the 1970 offerings if it were to keep pace with the national trend in giving to religion.

While total giving to religion shows some real gain during the last three years of the decade, giving to the mainline

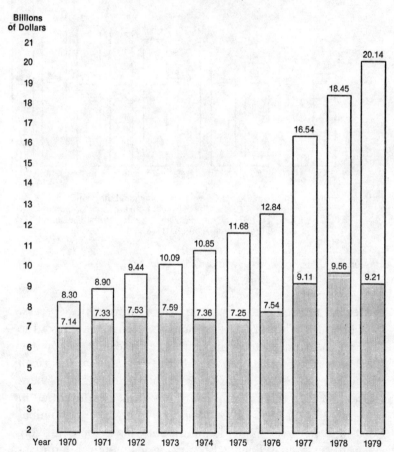

CHART 1. Total Annual Giving to Religion, 1970-79, in the United States in Billions of Dollars (Shaded Portion, 1967 = 100)

Source: *Giving, USA*

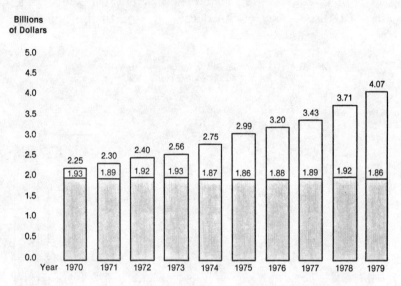

CHART 2. Total Annual Contributions, 1970-79, in
Eight Mainline Protestant Denominations*
in Billions of Dollars (Shaded Portion,
1967 = 100)

*Denominations: American Baptist Convention, American Lutheran Church,
Disciples of Christ, Episcopal Church, Lutheran Church in
America, United Church of Christ, United Methodist Church,
United Presbyterian Church, USA

Source: *Yearbook of American and Canadian Churches*

Protestant churches has remained stable during these years.
Chart 2 shows the total dollars (and the deflated value of the
dollars) contributed to eight mainline Protestant denominations, according to data reported in the *Yearbook of American
and Canadian Churches*. These eight denominations were
chosen because the 75 sample churches that are described in
more detail in Chapters V and VI are from these denominations, and because these denominations have comparatively
accurate systems of financial reporting. The eight denominations are reported as an aggregate total in order to average out

changes that may have resulted from reporting errors or brief turns of events that sometimes occur in a single denomination.

These eight denominations appear to keep abreast of inflation, but have not increased the amount of real income over the past decade. The increase in nominal contributions from 1970 to 1979 was 80.9 percent. During this same period the spendable weekly earnings of the U.S. labor force rose 96.1 percent (see Chart 3). Because income to churches comes principally from weekly contributions of persons, and because weekly contributions are related to spendable weekly earnings, the data provided by the U.S. Department of Labor on spendable weekly earnings is an important indicator for projecting income of Protestant churches. Income to churches and spendable weekly earnings have closely paralleled each other during the 1970s. (Compare Charts 2 and 3.) The parallel would be even more striking if the Southern Baptist Convention and the Church of the Nazarene, both of which had financial gains during the 1970s, had been included in addition to the eight denominations. These two are omitted here because no congregations were selected from these denominations for detailed study. In order to have kept pace with these eight denominations, the income in a local church would in 1979 need to be 1.8 times the income of 1970. And to have kept up with the increase in spendable weekly earnings, the 1979 offering income would need to be 2.2 times the 1970 offering.

The apparent "flat" trend during the 1970s hides the fact that some local churches faced sharp decline and others made marked financial gain. The particular configuration of factors causing economic gain or loss vary dramatically from parish to parish. In order for financial planners in local churches to determine how they fare economically, attention must be given to the buying power of this income, not just the actual amount of increase or decrease in dollars (a point that cannot be underscored enough).

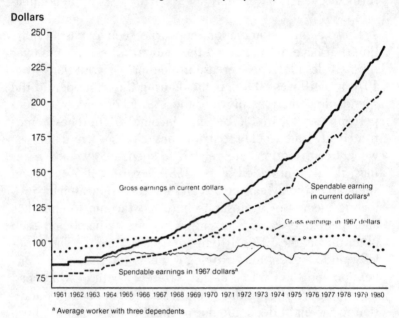

CHART 3. Total Private Gross and Spendable Weekly Earnings (Seasonally Adjusted)

Dollars

Gross earnings in current dollars

Spendable earning in current dollars[a]

Gross earnings in 1967 dollars

Spendable earnings in 1967 dollars[a]

[a] Average worker with three dependents

Source: Employment and Earnings, December 1980, U.S. Dept. of Labor.

Increasing numbers of clergy. Chart 4 shows the total number of clergy serving in the same eight Protestant denominations and the proportion of those clergy who are serving in local churches. While the total number has increased somewhat over the decade (5.59 percent), the number serving in parishes has remained almost constant, declining by 1.05 percent. Moreover, the number of persons enrolled in professional training for entrance into ministry in theological seminaries increased over the decade by 26 percent, according to records kept by the Association of Theological Schools.

These data suggest that clergy have had increasing difficulty finding parish employment during the 1970s.

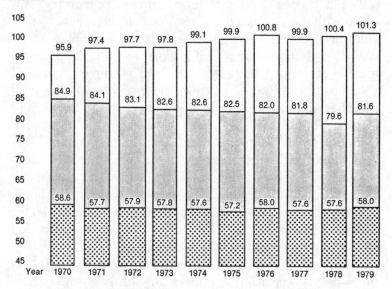

CHART 4. Total Number of Clergy (upper numbers), Total Number of Parishes (middle numbers), and Number of Clergy Serving Parishes (lower numbers) in Eight Mainline Protestant Denominations,* 1970-79

*Denominations: see Chart 2.

Source: *Yearbook of American and Canadian Churches*

Parishes have enjoyed, so to speak, a buyers' market for clergy services, while the number of opportunities for clergy to move to new pastoral positions has declined. This trend, identified early in the decade, has been monitored throughout the past 10 years by concerned observers. The number of clergy available for placement may drop by the end of the 1980s, largely because the clergy who entered the ministry in the 1940s and 1950s are becoming eligible for retirement. Also, many theological seminaries are experiencing a rise in the average age of people studying for entrance into the ministry because of the number of "second career" ordinands. Persons starting their career in ministry in their late 40s and 50s will obviously have fewer years of service, thereby reducing even further the number of persons available for serving local churches as pastors in the late 1980s and 1990s.

The increasing number of persons trained in ministry combined with the financial crunch of inflation and recession provide the occasion for many congregations to reorganize the way they provide professional leadership. In fact, while the number of clergy potentially available to be employed by local churches has continued to grow, the proportion of the local churches' annual budgets allocated to pastors' salaries and expenses has declined during the 1970s in the 75 sample churches, from 34.6 percent in 1970 to 29.2 percent in 1979. This reduction has been accomplished in a variety of ways, the long-range consequences of which may not have been anticipated by the leaders who made the decisions. Some churches have reduced the size of their staffs, usually in ways that appear to be making little change in the service provided by the pastor(s), but that can realize a savings: not replacing part-time staff, extended interim periods when a pastoral vacancy occurs, replacing full-time staff with part-time staff or nonprofessional staff or volunteers, and employing the head pastor on a less than 100 percent basis. One church studied for this report went from three full-time pastors to one during the 1970s, solely to save costs. Each of the above staff-reduction strategies has been followed by more than one of the 75 sample churches. In addition there are strategies to keep pastors' salaries down: offering pay increments less than the rate of inflation, seeking pastors with less experience, or a lower pay scale when a vacancy occurs. This latter strategy is especially enticing to churches considering employing a second-career pastor who recently graduated from seminary. Because of the age of the prospective pastor, they appear to be getting more experience than they actually are.

The present oversupply of clergy makes the above strategies work, but they may be ill advised. Churches need to build their pastoral staffs, even if the staff consists of only one part-time pastor, according to the kinds of expertise and service they require in order to accomplish desired results. Short-term savings in pastoral salary may increase costs or contribute to the church's failure in the long run. If the abovementioned strategies for cutting the amount of money spent for pastoral services are under consideration, church leaders would appropriately raise such questions as the following before making final decisions. What kinds of personal characteristics and professional skills do they want the pastor(s) to have? How much does it cost to employ pastors with these personal characteristics and professional skills? What would be the consequences of not having such characteristics and skills available to the congregation? The more specificity in answering questions such as these, the better. It is better to say "We want a preacher who can communicate with a congregation of blue-collar workers" than simply to say "We want a good preacher." Better yet would be the answer, "We want a preacher who can communicate with blue-collar workers about their domestic struggles and their attempts to make their faith apply to their everyday work lives." If this is the kind of pastor needed, someone who cannot do it, even though he or she requires less salary, is no bargain.

Notwithstanding the changes in the ways congregations staff their programs, the one-pastor-one-church model continues to be normative in the minds of most local church leaders, and will probably continue to be the usual pattern. Innovations, such as cooperative groups of pastors who sell their services on a contract basis to several churches or the extensive use of trained volunteers to assume some of the responsibilities traditionally assigned to the pastor, have made only minimal inroads into the normal pattern of staffing in the 75 sample churches.

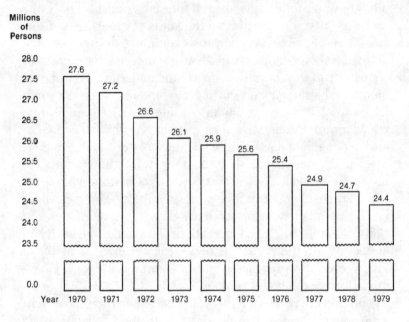

*Denominations: see Chart 2.

Source: *Yearbook of American and Canadian Churches*

Membership decline. Chart 5 plots the decline in member-ship reported by the eight denominations during the 1970s. The loss is 11.4 percent, or more than 3 million persons. While losses of membership may be expected to have nega-tive effects on local church economics, the loss of members may not be great among active attenders and persons who contribute financial support. There is not a drop in giving commensurate with the drop in membership (compare Chart 5 and Chart 2). Alternatively, remaining members may have increased their giving to make up for losses. Church attendance appears to follow the same pattern of loss. According to surveys published in the *Gallup Opinion Index*, church attendance is stable or down in the same eight Protestant denominations. When all Protestant groups were aggregated, however, a modest increase in percent attendance was noted by Gallup. (See Table 1.)

The financial implications of this membership loss are staggering at face value. Three million members, at the average per-capita rate ($165), would contribute almost a half billion dollars per year. Had these eight denominations not lost these members, their income would have increased by almost 8 percent, after inflation effects were removed, during the 1970s. The membership loss in these denominations may be accounted for by death of members, transfer of members out-

TABLE 1
Per Capita* Contributions for Selected Protestant Denominations, 1979–80

	Total Contribution	Local Church Expenses	Benevolence
American Baptist Convention	144.31	$122.45	$ 21.86
American Lutheran Church	160 56	132.84	27.72
Church of the Nazarene	454.72	395.51	59.21
Disciples of Christ	186.90	160.59	26.31
Episcopal Church	182.09	153.49	28.60
Lutheran Church in America	157.16	127.25	29.91
Seventh-Day Adventist	695.57	212.71	482.86
Southern Baptist Convention	182.44	152.96	29.48
United Church of Christ	185.80	160.43	25.37
United Methodist	154.77	118.94	35.83
United Presbyterian Church, USA	291.27	241.83	49.44

*The amounts given include children of members as well as confirmed members.

SOURCE: Yearbook of American and Canadian Churches, 1982.

side the eight denominations, and removal of members by local church action. These three channels of membership loss simply outpaced the number of new members.

Per-capita average annual contributions vary from denomination to denomination, as shown in Table 2. This table may be used by church leaders in two ways. First, it can be used to see how their own rate of giving compares with that of their own or other denominations. Second, it may be used to provide multipliers to estimate roughly the financial implications of membership loss or gain.

The persons leaving the churches' membership may be contributing at a different rate from those joining, which can make enormous differences between reality and the gross calculation made by using Table 2. Church leaders need to be aware of these variations. One pastor of a northeastern church (included in the research reported in this volume) observed that when one of the major contributors to his church retired and moved to Florida, a common occurrence in that particular congregation, five new families would need to be recruited in order to have an equal amount in contributions. This pastor's discovery illustrates the need for local church financial planners to monitor characteristics of both the people joining the church and the people leaving the church. Using the model presented in detail in Chapter I, Diagram 1, it is possible to

TABLE 2

Church Attendance During Average Week, 1970 and 1976, by Protestant Denomination

	PERSONS WHO ATTEND	
	1970	1976
All Protestants	38%	40%
Baptists	39	38
Methodists	38	34
Lutherans	34	41
Presbyterians	34	34
Episcopalians	29	34

SOURCE: Gallup Opinion Index, Report No. 145, p. 32

70

identify trends in membership gains and losses beyond a simple head count. These data provide an important indicator of the congregation's future financial health.

Decline in number of congregations. Many churches closed their doors during the 1970s. The net loss in the eight denominations was 3.9 percent, or 3,341 congregations. Chart 4 reflects this gradual decline. The actual closing of local churches, however, appears on the surface to be of little financial consequence to the denominations. By the time the closing occurs, there are probably too few members and too little money involved to have obvious effects. The big losses, if there were any, were recorded as the dying churches declined in the years preceding the closing.

Three types of disbanded congregations were identified as part of the present research.

- Old congregations disband when they have lost their traditional constituencies and have been unsuccessful in attracting new constituencies. In most cases the traditional constituencies have moved away. In some cases, the actual community has been destroyed by urban renewal or closing of industry in small towns. In other cases, people moving into the area are not attracted to the church, or come in insufficient numbers to support the church's program.
- Newer churches, started in the 1950s and 1960s, fail when they are unable to establish a constituency that can sustain them. (See the case study "Never Say Die" in Appendix I.)
- Local churches, new and old, sometimes close because of church fights or schisms. The closing usually does not immediately follow the schism, because a residual membership continues the church, at least for a while. If the residual constituency is insufficiently large to support a membership and new members are not forthcoming, the church faces closing.

71

The financial implications of church closings for nearby surviving churches are several and complex. Very few churches close with no membership and no financial resource at the time of closing. Most congregations vote, when closing is imminent, to merge with another congregation, as is the case with St. John's and the church called LUCK described in Appendix I. Some mergers work well and others work not at all, probably depending on the degree to which the joining congregations share similar interpretations of the new church's desired results and a variety of demographic factors. Some mergers are poisoned by ill feelings generated in the months and years of decline preceding the actual closing. Thus, while surviving congregations may attract new members from disbanding congregations, poorly timed approaches to the closing church can generate much counterproductive conflict. The case of Bethany United Methodist Church illustrates the problem. Bethany was located across the parking lot from another church of the same denomination. A denominational merger in 1946 had made the two congregations members of the same denomination. Over the years there were many conversations and several formal proposals for merger. Bethany, the smaller and poorer of the two, consistently voted against merger. Each time the vote was taken, Bethany would lose more members from among those who favored merger, thereby weakening Bethany even further. When merger finally came in 1980, few members joined the church across the parking lot. Some went to an independent evangelistic church that made special overtures to Bethany's members, even to the extent of salvaging the large oil painting over Bethany's altar, given without charge to the independent church by the demolition contractor. Others transferred membership to one of the several United Methodist churches in the city. Still others have not joined any church. Bethany's circumstances are repeated in many other local churches, which, because of the pain of their slow death, fail to save the main purposes or goals for which the congregation stood, let

72

alone financial resources that might be used for other purposes by a surviving group.

Summary. The 1970s were for the eight denominations (from which the 75 sample congregations were drawn for this study) years of stability or slight decline. The momentum that produced growth in the 1950s and 1960s had been lost. Buying power remained unchanged while the number of clergy increased. The number of members and congregations declined. The 75 churches that provided financial data for this book need to be seen against this general demographic backdrop, as do any other churches that use this book. Of course, there are weaknesses in drawing inferences using this broad picture. It masks a good deal of variation from denomination to denomination. Moreover, emphasis on these statistics implies that growth in finances and number of members is a universally desired goal, which is in fact not the case for some church groups. They may have objectives that are better served by small groups of people and require limited finances. One pastor of a church included in the sample observed, "The most significant event is the decision to remain in the city despite rapidly changing neighborhoods and loss of members to the suburbs. We have a ministry here and intend to stay." The 1970s appear to have been a time of significant roll-cleaning for these denominations too. Churches that have inactive members on their rolls are motivated to remove their names, especially if the money required of the local churches by denominations is based on formulas using numbers of members.

CHAPTER IV

The Local Church as
an Economic System

Many books have been written about religion and money. In the early and mid-nineteenth century, church leaders began to reawaken to the theological significance of money and to integrity in money management for the life of the congregation. As a result, the modern emphasis on stewardship was born, giving rise to the stewardship bureaucracies in twentieth-century American Protestant denominations. Titles of nineteenth-century books on stewardship—*Gold and the Gospel, A Plea for the Lord's Portion of a Christian's Wealth,* and *Christian Beneficence*—reflect the concerns of the progenitors of the contemporary stewardship movement for tithing, charity, and ethics of the use of money.

In the twentieth century, the number of books written about stewardship has expanded greatly, so much so that further study of church finances may seem unnecessary.

There are, after all, books that explain the theology of Christian stewardship from many perspectives, books that present plans for fund raising in local churches, books that report financial trends for denominations, books that deal with money management for churches, books that detail accounting procedures, books that critique the "financial empire" of religion, and books that deal with special problems of church finances such as taxes and real-estate holdings. Moreover, a prodigious number of pamphlets, visual resources, and other materials is produced annually by the denominational departments of stewardship. A selected bibliography of these materials is provided at the back of this book.

This book differs from these others principally because of its perspective on the local church as an economic system. Basically, the model alluded to in Chapter I and explained more fully here provides a way to interpret what a local church is trying to do financially, how it goes about minding its financial affairs, and what helps or hinders it in achieving financial health. The model presents the local church as an objective-accomplishing organization in a specific social and economic context, called here the demographic niche. Viewed in this way, the local church is an economic entity that acquires a variety of resources (goods and services) in order to produce desired results that constitute the ministry and mission of the congregation. The benefits of these results are consumed by the congregation's members and others in the community and beyond. Moreover, evaluation of results serves as one basis for making further financial decisions: How much will we give? Who will be hired? What will be purchased?

The research data presented in Chapters V to VII and the case studies in Appendix I are intended to illustrate the local church economic model and to demonstrate the value of elementary economic modeling for planning local church finance.

Some Assumptions and Definitions

Before elaborating the model further, two assumptions underlying it and its use need to be identified and critiqued: the assumption that the idea of economic and social exchange is appropriate for use in describing local churches, and the assumption that people are rational in making decisions about church finances. The idea of demographic niche also needs to be defined.

People engage in any particular financial exchange—for example, paying money for a piece of clothing—because they expect what they buy to be worth what they pay. There is an equality in the exchange. Likewise, people may enter into friendships and social associations because they expect doing so to be rewarding. The relationship may be internally rewarding, as in a love relationship, or may bring external rewards, such as valued advice from a pastor or help on a project from a neighbor.

There are some logical and theological problems in assuming that people in a local church operate on the basis of economic and social exchange. While the act of a local church paying its electric bill, for example, can readily be understood as an economic exchange, the act of a member contributing money to the church may or may not be governed by her or his interest in direct or even indirect rewards. Moral and theological values influence the decision to give, as do irrational forces. Moreover, for theological reasons, much of the preaching about giving in the church is without expectation of reward—in the words of Longfellow, "The greatest grace is a gift, perhaps, in that it anticipates no return." Because everything we have already belongs to God, and because God has given us in Christ the greatest possible gift, there can be no reciprocity, no exchange. On the surface, this kind of theological position seems to preclude application of the ideas of economic and social exchange to many local church financial operations, especially in regard to giving.

An argument for the restricted use of social and economic

exchange in relation to church finances can be made, however. People give to the church for a great variety of reasons, as elaborated below, but in part because they expect their gifts to result in the accomplishment of ministries in their local churches, whatever those ministries may be. Fulfillment of this expectation can be reasonably construed as reward. They expect a kind of return on their gift: the satisfaction that the ministry is being accomplished.

To be sure, some members give and work selflessly for their church without thought of reward, without expecting gratitude, or perhaps without even expecting their efforts to be well used to accomplish their church's ministry. These are innocent saints, and saints are few. Other members give and work selflessly, but require some incentive, if only to know they are appreciated and that their work is worthwhile. As a result, concepts of economic and social exchange can be helpful in understanding not only the obvious economic transactions of a local church, but also why people give and what they expect in return. In a sense, an informed contributor requires insight into whether the money is used to accomplish intended purposes.

The second assumption, rationality, supposes that if the goals of a congregation are articulated in clear, accomplishable tasks, members will seek to accomplish these goals subject to the availability of resources. In actual situations, financial decisions are often made on impulse by persons with little or no awareness of the congregation's goals. (See Chapter V, for example, for the reasons why some congregations who were asked to participate could not be included in this study.) One congregation not included in the study considered its main ministry to be among the city's poor people. When its building was destroyed by fire, the church council used the insurance money to build a similar structure on the same site, notwithstanding the fact that most of the original building had fallen into disuse. That was not a particularly rational decision. The model discussed herein will be most helpful to those churches that do articulate their goals and use them to guide decision making. Whether the level of rationality in doing this is sufficiently high to make use of this model has to be determined on a church-by-church basis.

Diagram 2 presents the model itself in graphic form. The boxes represent the key elements of the model, and the circled letters represent key decision-making points. It is a dynamic model with no starting or stopping points. It reflects how many people making decisions about the economics of a local church fit together in a system that is affected by the surrounding environment (demographic niche). In what follows, each element of the model is elaborated along with the decisions that precede it. While it is not the simplest model of local church finances that could be drawn, neither is it extremely complicated.

In the diagram, each key element in the system is shown to be affected by the constraints of the demographic niche as well as having some effect on the niche. The arrows pointing toward each other are meant to convey this idea. Aspects of a local church's demographic niche include the population from which the church draws members and their income, the persons or firms or agencies from which the church purchases goods and services (including the denomination), banks and financial advisers, and the community immediately surrounding the church. In short, the demographic niche includes everyone who gives or sells anything to the church or gets, buys, or benefits in any way from the church. Some particularly important constraints of the demographic niche on each element in a local church's financial system are listed in what follows.

The demographic niche is not the same for any two churches, even if they are across the street from each other. For example, if a factory closes, one congregation may have drastically reduced income while another may notice no change at all. The difference results from the first church

DIAGRAM 2

Flow of Church Finances

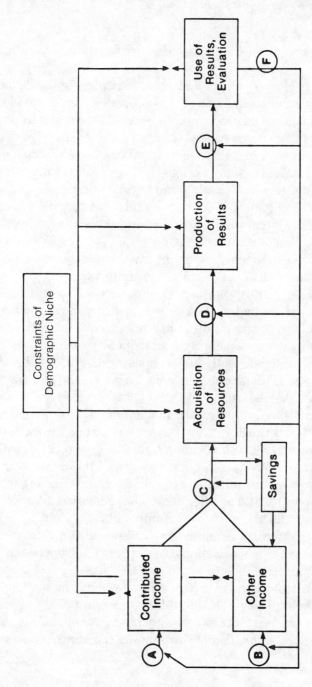

A Decisions of individuals and families to contribute time and money.
B Decisions about managing endowments, sponsoring bazaars, applying for foundation grants, etc.
C Decisions about budget construction, what resources are needed.
D Decisions about how to use the resources acquired to accomplish the desired results.
E Decision of persons and groups to use the resulting ministries, and evaluative decisions about the worth of the ministry.
F Decisions about how to use the evaluations to make future financial decisions.

having many members employed at the factory and the other few.

The idea of the demographic niche is simple, but the details of even a small congregation's niche are elaborate. Skilled church financial planners need to be able to pick out important parts of the niche quickly, to monitor them with reasonable accuracy, and to make financial decisions informed by their own insights. Many businesses do this kind of modeling using computers that enable them to predict how changes in their niche will affect their system and what changes in one part of their system will do to other parts of the system. While such modeling in churches is only in the very beginning stages of development, important insights can be gained by thinking about the church's finances in this way.

The value of this approach is illustrated in some typical problems. The members in a church made up of retired persons want a young pastor who can attract youth. But there are few youth in the community from which the church draws members, and no youth in the congregation. The church members misunderstand their demographic niche and fail to recognize that the change they want to make will probably not bring about the desired result. In another church, the members want very much to attract new members and work hard for few results. The ethnic group traditionally associated with that church is declining in the community, and the members have not sought to relate to new ethnic groups moving into the community. Still another church has an important opportunity for ministry in its community, but does not take it because of the costs. Members are unaware that a sister congregation in a neighboring town would help if the opportunity were explained to them.

Two characteristics of a local church's demographic niche may be helpful in predicting future financial health for the congregation. First, the growth or decline in population of the neighborhood immediately surrounding the church—for example, the zip-code area—may be predictive of growth or decline in membership. Even if the congregation's membership is drawn from a much larger territory, the population in the zip code or a group of census tracts (provided by the U.S. Bureau of Census) surrounding the church are more likely to reflect accurately the trends in membership than are larger aggregations. Second, the growth or decline in income of people living in the area surrounding the local church is helpful in predicting local church income. Local church leaders might consult with a demographer or census-data expert in a nearby university to get the information they need for comparisons.

Before proceeding to the elaboration of Diagram 2, questions about the theological appropriateness of using a systems model to analyze local church financial operations need to be raised. There are two valid objections to conceptualizing the church as a system. First, not everything a local church wants or needs to be or do is programmatic. The experience of forgiving and of being forgiven, the experience of ecstasy, the dawning of insight, revelation, the feeling of awe, the discovery of beauty, and the resurgence of hope after despair are all examples of desired results that are not fundamentally programmatic in nature. The best that planned programs can do toward achieving these desired results is to create an environment and a set of circumstances in which they are believed likely to occur—places, times, leaders, and materials. Moreover, these desired results may occur without any program, and programs may actually impede their realization. Second, programs and systems sometimes produce unexpected, unintended results, some of which are good, a kind of serendipity of planning, but some of which are bad. Efforts to help people experience forgiveness may result only in increasing their guilt and pain. Attempts to encourage insight through preaching may result in hearers being more confused. Building an addition to the sanctuary to accommodate more worshipers may result in losing the intimacy of the smaller sanctuary that had attracted the present worshipers in the first place.

The systems model presented in this chapter is intended for use only with those aspects of church life that are programmatic—that is, which require expenditures of time, money, and other scarce resources. Each program, whether it be teaching sixth graders, building a new building, commissioning a work of art, or paying for a missionary activity, needs to be defended theologically on the basis of the worthiness of the intended desired result, and defended practically on the basis of the effectiveness of the program in producing the desired result. Systems models can help with the latter, but not with the former. Moreover, systems analysis of church programs can sometimes actually help in identifying unanticipated, unexpected results, because it requires using a broader perspective than often is the case when local church financial decisions are made.

The model elaborated below is not a tight mathematical system reduceable to formulas, although further development may lead in that direction. It is intended only as a tool to help church leaders understand and improve their planning and the consequences of their planning. The lettered sections correspond to the lettered decision points in Diagram 2.

A. *Contributed income and decisions about it.* In order to pursue the economic analogy in the study of local congregations, some elaboration of the model is necessary. The church must go into the marketplace and acquire the necessary resources for accomplishing the desired results. The cost of producing the results equals the price the churches must pay for goods and services in the marketplace, plus the energy represented by contributed services of volunteers, plus overhead (constant operational costs of the church). These expenses are covered by several sources of income, but principally by the regular contributions of members. In addition to cash income, the volunteered services and materials contributed by members are also major economic assets of congregations. Often contributions in kind—paint and painters, for example—directly save money that would have been needed to purchase goods in the open market. Measurements of the worth of in-kind contributions are not easily accomplished because there is no way to establish their value. Persons making these gifts in kind, however, probably expect a return for their investment of time and energy in the same way as people who contribute only money.

Although motivation for giving is not a major aspect of the inquiry on which this book is based, some attention needs to be given to motivation at this point. The assumption in the model is that people often expect some fair exchange for the time and money they give to the church, even if only that the church's ministry is being accomplished in the best possible ways given the constraints of the demographic niche. There are many other reasons why people give away money and time. Exploration of some of these reasons can clarify how the idea of economic and social exchange can be applied to church finances. First, a bandit could rob them. While this may be seen as an exchange (your money for your life), physical or psychological coercion seems inappropriately included in the notion of exchange as discussed here. Obviously, coercion has been used in some instances to raise money for the church, as in the notion of requiring gifts to avoid damnation. The old joke about the preacher whose calling card says he is a "fire insurance salesman" reflects an undercurrent of coercion in church giving. Second, people may donate money because their conscience demands, for example, that they help the poor through the church without expecting any form of gratitude. The idea of exchange is germane here only insofar as people want to be sure the poor benefit from their gift and their own conscience needs are met. Similarly, people may give because their conscience demands they return part of their income to God, a motive that sometimes lies behind tithing. Third, people may squander their money, giving it away to anyone, including the church, because of irrational drives. The idea of exchange does not accurately apply here either. Fourth, a person may give because he or she expects differential gratitude in return for the gift—perhaps naming the church for a large gift or placing a name plate in a hymnal for a small gift—and the giving would cease if the church failed to react with such expressions of gratitude. Obviously, in such cases the idea of exchange applies explicitly. Yet theological objections could be raised about this motivation because of its self-centered character. Fifth, people may give because they are committed to the purpose for which the gift will be used. The gift is rewarded because of the contributor's satisfaction of seeing the purpose well accomplished. In this regard, giving to the church is much like paying for one's children's education or medical care. It contributes to the accomplishment of purposes that are collectively shared. Sixth, people may give to the church because there is a specific fee for services they receive. For example, fees are sometimes charged for counseling or performing marriages. In the rapidly growing cult of Scientology, adherents are charged specific fees as they advance from stage to stage in that group's scheme of religious growth.

In some instances, therefore, a person's decisions to give to the church fit the model's assumption of an economic and social exchange; in other cases they do not. The fact that the assumption does not hold in certain circumstances, however, does not invalidate its use as a tool for analyzing the church's finances. Church leaders need to ask what, if anything, people expect in return for the time and money they give to the church. If, after serious theological reflection, there is a consensus answer to this question among the congregation's members, that answer may be the clearest statement of the congregation's desired results. Without knowing what members expect in return for their contributions, church leaders might plan the budget and carry out the church's financial transactions in such a way as to undercut their primary source of income.

B. Other income and decisions about its management. Other revenues come to the church from denominational subsidies, interest on endowments, rentals of church properties, profits from church enterprises, and direct fees for services rendered. While in the average congregation the amount realized from these sources is small, the decisions made about them are highly important and often neglected. Does the local church need the maximum amount of income from the endowment for subsidy of the present program, or does it need to reinvest the income for a future project? Will a fund-raising project—a bazaar or bingo night—produce income commensurate with the money invested in the project plus the energies of volunteers plus overhead?

If the church has a small endowment, something under a million dollars, investment strategies are complicated yet crucial to overall income. The church can either manage its own investments, have a secular institution such as the trust department of a bank invest its money, or find a cooperative investment program with other religious groups. Each approach has its strengths and weaknesses. If the church invests its own money, it maintains control over its assets but often at the cost of poor management. Local church leaders cannot be expected to keep up to date on all investment opportunities. Moreover, the advantage gained by investing large sums of money is lost when a church manages its own investment portfolio. If a secular investment agency is employed, the advantages of professional advice must be balanced with the disadvantages of large financial institutions' lack of awareness of the economic needs of local churches. Cooperative investing with other churches provides some correction to the problems of the other two strategies, but is a comparatively new venture and is unavailable to a great many congregations.

Managing a medium-sized or small endowment presents one of the most important challenges to local church finances. Much more needs to be learned about how to do it. Leaders of congregations that presently have no endowment need to consider how they would invest such money if they did have it. Potential benefactors are more likely to provide bequests if they are convinced their money will be managed effectively.

C. Acquisition of resources and decisions about budget construction. Diagram 2 shows income being changed into results by passing through an intermediate step called Acquisition of Resources. Income is used to purchase the materials, skills, and services necessary to accomplish its desired results. At decision point C on the diagram, church leaders decide what will be purchased and how much money, if any, will be held in reserve as savings.

All resources acquired—the services of a pastor, fuel, secretarial services, choir music—are the instruments thought to be the best available for accomplishing the results desired by the congregation. Debates that arise at budget-construction time about what is increased and what is cut are of two kinds. First, there are debates about whether the particular resource in question will do the job of producing the desired result— for example, will hiring a minister of evangelism really increase membership? Second, debates arise about the worth of the intended result—for example, do we really want and need to increase membership in order to be faithful to our calling? As a result the best church budgets, as indicated in Appendix II, point directly to the goals or desired results of a congregation. Most if not all the church's goals can be inferred from the budget items.

Resources are instruments for accomplishing the theological results desired by the congregation. The purchase of new choir robes, for example, is an intermediate resource that in turn leads to the more final product of a worshipful setting for Sunday services, which presumably leads to even more ultimate results of faith and inspiration. Money given to mission projects can be understood as funds used to purchase fulfillment of the congregation's goals in ministry.

D. The production of results and decisions about what results to produce. Economists customarily define an industry in terms of its results, the production or provision of particular goods or services. Hence the references to the auto industry, the housing industry, and so on. In the service industry (health, education, arts, government services) the results are more difficult to define, yet this definition is necessary to assess the effectiveness of the industry. This definitional task is especially difficult for religious groups, because there is no clear consensus on what the "product" of religious groups is or should be. The ultimate results of church groups might be described as faith, or personal dignity, or salvation, or righteousness, or justice and peace, but these theological results defy easy economic or empirical descriptions. On another level, there are several more observable activities in local churches that may be described as results: credal assent, personal religious experience, church attendance, attendance at organizational activities, religious knowledge, personal devotional life, care for the infirm or bereaved. Results are more easily measured among these more observable activities carried out by the churches and their members, but even then serious problems need to be overcome. Persons who define the outcomes in solely qualitative theological terms, however, will find the measurements lacking in understanding and depth.

At still a third level, the specific use made by a congregation of the resources it purchases or otherwise acquires can be understood in a sense as economic results. The amount of volunteer time given to worship preparation, the amount of money given to mission projects, the amount of the pastor's time given to counseling, all reflect results. These are, in fact, the principal results discussed in this volume. While the theological outcomes mentioned above are related to the economic results, they are distinguishable from them. The economic results are derived from the theological.

Results, economic and theological, differ from congregation to congregation, and most congregations may be described as multiproduct firms. For some congregations, the principal product may be a particular quality of worship service designed to meet the needs of blue-collar workers and their families. For others, it may be that competent counseling of suburban families is a valued product. For still others, the main product is the preservation of a tradition in liturgy. And for others, the principal product is feeding and clothing the poor. For all these, the ultimate product may be described as service to God and people. Results of a congregation's activities may, however, be unanticipated, even antithetical, to the announced beliefs of members. In many congregations, for example, there is an expressed belief in equality among people of different races; yet the *Gallup Opinion Index* reported in 1977 that Martin Luther King's observation that Sunday-morning worship was the most segregated hour of the week was as true in 1977 as when King said it a decade earlier. The result is not consistent with the announced beliefs.

The way a local church changes its resources into desired results may be described as a process of production, and to the extent that the process involves finances, it is an economic process. There are many processes that any particular congregation uses, but all of them transform resources into results. On one hand, the church may be seeking deliberately to maximize the accomplishment of a particular set of tasks: build or maintain buildings by purchasing brick and paint or by employing a contractor, increase attendance and/or membership by employing more staff people, teach doctrine by training people to teach catechisms, convert and baptize more people, or preserve its heritage by publishing its history. On the other hand, the church may be seeking to maximize the accomplishment of a particular quality of relationships: maintain friendly relationships by providing a coffee hour, insure member satisfaction with clergy or church programs by hiring a consultant to evaluate them, demonstrate care for others by contributing to mission, promote peace by contributing to nuclear-freeze promotions, or develop members' personal potential by special adult-training programs. The strategies actually followed reflect what the congregation and/or the financial leaders understand to be the desired results and an effective way of accomplishing them given the limits of available resources. How does the purchase of visitor-recognition cards help people to feel welcome? How does the purchase of janitorial services yield effective maintenance of the building, which in turn fosters people's feelings of reverence? How does money spent for the pastor's continuing education produce better or more extensive counseling services? How does money spent for food for congregational dinners translate into friendly relationships among members? How does money contributed to the denomination result in disaster relief, or in hungry people being fed, or in people hearing the gospel, or in denominations being governed? These production questions stem from the perspective of an economic model of a local church.

E. Decisions about the use of results and evaluation. Who benefits when the church does something?

Results desired and produced by a local church are used by the members, the community around the church, the denomination, and anyone else who benefits (or suffers) as the consequence of the church's productive activity. These people decide to attend worship or not, to listen to a sermon or not, to seek counseling from the pastor or not, to accept the congregation's gifts of food or money or clothing or not, to experience a personal fulfillment of what they believe God wants them to be or do or not. In a sense, the denomination decides whether to receive benevolence funds from the local church, although a refusal to receive them is highly unlikely. Nevertheless, the local church does produce services that people seek and use. On the one hand, individuals may make conscious decisions every time they choose to use some one of the church's results. On the other hand, many members as a matter of personal commitment let their church decide what religious behavior is appropriate and what services they are expected to use, as with individuals who have never missed church school for forty years no matter what the church school offered.

Why people choose to use some of the church's results and not others is of concern not only to the leaders who create and manage the church's program, but also to the financial leaders. Financial leaders need to know who makes up the constituencies for each result produced. Is the constituency growing or declining? What part of the cost of producing the result can or should constituents pay for through their contributions (or even direct fees for benefits received)? If the people who pay for the result are not the same people who are the principal beneficiaries of the result, are both groups' expectations about the result compatible?

For example, the primary constituency of children's worship is, of course, composed of children, but the adults (parents and nonparents alike) make up an important secondary constituency who in fact pay for this particular result. The adults' expectations for children's worship may in fact impede the effectiveness of children's worship for the children. An announcement in a church newsletter illustrates the problem: "The Worship Committee requests adults to refrain from laughing at children's responses during Children's Time in the worship service. Laughter distracts the children from the

90

intent of this portion of worship, tending to turn their participation into a performance." Some adults may be seeking such a performance, however, and may find in the remarks of the children a humor that is spiritually refreshing. Hence they laugh, want to attend worship, and want to support the church financially. The problem in the church making the announcement about Children's Time, therefore, is not of concern only for leaders of the Children's Time program, but also for the financial leaders. Any time there is a conflict of expectations about results, financial leaders are directly involved in its consequences. In this case, if the adults' true desire is for the children to worship and their laughter interrupts this, it is hoped they will cease laughing and the matter will be resolved. (Children, after all, rarely laugh at the things adults say during worship, and when they do adults are usually not amused.) With such a resolution, the children's, the adults', and the Children's Time leaders' expectations of the results are reasonably compatible.

In some cases the constituents for particular results are not obvious to church leaders, and their identification may help elicit additional financial support for the church's activity. A large, prominently located inner-city church recently paid over $10,000 to paint its exterior. The primary constituency for this result is the membership whose place of worship is preserved and beautified. The members also paid for the improvement, but the surrounding community as a whole benefited. Property values were perceived to be improved, and some landlords were motivated to paint and otherwise clean up their buildings. A fire-insurance executive, observing that his company would benefit because the overall community improvements would mean less risk of fire, made a contribution to the church to help defray the costs of painting. This sequence of events illustrates the interrelationships between decisions made by the church's financial leaders and the larger demographic niche.

Evaluation is linked closely with the use of the church's

results. The constituents of each result do the real evaluating. If there is merit in what is called evaluation in local churches—groups of leaders who assess the worth of the church's programs using whatever data and opinions they can amass—it must in fact derive from the opinions of the people who use the church's results. What is the value of the children's worship to the children? What is the significance of the money sent for a mission project in the Third World to the recipients? Of what importance is the counseling service to the persons counseled? What assessments do the worshipers make of the lenten services? Questions such as these elicit the first and most important level of evaluation.

F. Introducing change: decisions about the future. When the leaders have collected the evaluations, then decisions about what changes are required in the various parts of the financial operation need to be made. In Diagram 2, the arrows pass through the circle labeled *F* to all the other decision points. The evaluation of a particular result may require changes at any one or several of the other decision points. For example, suppose the leaders discovered the counseling load of the pastor was heavily burdened with serious problems about which the pastor had little or no expertise. The leaders could intervene at any of the decision points labeled *A* through *E* on Diagram 2. They could limit the constituency for the counseling service (point *E*) by restricting the service to members. They could modify the desired result (point *D*) by having the pastor counsel only persons with less serious problems, referring others to professional help in the community. They could decide to provide more resources for counseling (point *C*) by employing additional staff or by supporting the pastor in developing increased skill through continuing education. They may need to seek additional income (points *A* and *B*) to support whatever changes they choose to introduce. Of course, not all the options they could choose are exhausted above. The point is that the leaders can respond at any point in the model with the decisions most appropriate for them. Moreover, the model can be used to help leaders identify their options within the constraining limits of their financial resources.

CHAPTER V

Research Design

Data from several congregations have been collected both to illustrate the model and to provide insights for local church financial planners. In this chapter the congregations are described, the plan for research is outlined, and some problems encountered in collecting the data are discussed.

Description of the Sample Congregations

The 75 congregations that provided data reported herein are located in New England, middle Atlantic, midwestern, and southern states, in an area extending from Massachusetts to Alabama and as far west as Indiana. One congregation from the West (Arizona) was also included. Congregations were selected from diverse community settings, using a typology developed by Douglas Walrath. (See Appendix III for a description of each type.) Table 3 shows the types of communities and the number of congregations in each type. There is a disproportionate number of urban churches because the researchers expected, on the basis of preliminary explorations, that urban churches were facing the most acute financial difficulties. Moreover, the greatest difficulty in obtaining data was anticipated in the inner-city churches.

Membership also ranges in the sample congregations from a low of 63 to a high of 1,927 persons in 1979, with an average of 572. Average attendance is only 184, ranging from a low of 58 to a high of 491.

The amounts expended in 1979 by these churches vary from a low of $21,527 to a high of $401,762, and the median expenditure is $95,201 (average expenditure: $90,786).

The denominational affiliations of the sample congregations are as follows: United Church of Christ, 24; United Methodist, 14; United Presbyterian, 10; Protestant Episcopal, 9; Baptist, 6; Lutheran, 4; Disciples of Christ, 3; other, 5. Two of the congregations are black.

Nature of the Data Requested

Data requested from congregations are appropriate for describing the detailed fiscal history of these congregations for the past 15 years, along with some long-range data in five-year

TABLE 3
Number of Sample Congregations in Each Community Type ($N = 75$)

Midtown locale	9
Inner-city locale	4
Inner-urban neighborhood	10
Outer-urban neighborhood	8
City suburbs	5
Metropolitan suburbs	9
Fringe suburbs	2
Fringe village	8
Fringe settlements	2
Independent city	5
Rural village	10
Rural settlement	3

periods from 1950 to 1965. The research plan calls for data that would be appropriate for illustrating the model presented in Chapter IV. Income and expenses are broken into categories to allow detailed analysis. Information about the number of employees, their professional status, and their salaries is also assembled, as well as data about the number of volunteers used in providing the services of the congregations. Opinions of the financial leaders of the congregations are also collected. Eight leaders in each congregation were asked to complete opinion questionnaires. Four hundred forty of the possible 600 leaders (73 percent) responded to questions about the present and future economic situation in their congregations.

Although congregations were encouraged to complete the forms as nearly as possible by themselves, staff assistance was provided by the research team to all asking for it. An accountant was employed to provide control over the consistency of reporting from congregation to congregation. Data from three congregations were rejected because the congregations' accounting processes were insufficiently detailed to allow the necessary research distinctions.

Problems Encountered in Obtaining the Data

As anticipated by the researchers, data about finances were not easily obtained from the congregations. Some congregations keep detailed records for only two or three years; others have insufficient records even for current years. Smaller churches, especially those in rural areas, maintain no records at all, prepare no reports other than oral reports of the treasurer, and even throw away check stubs after a few years. In some cases, expenditures are left largely to the discretion of the treasurer of the congregation, who guards the confidentiality of the financial records as a sacred trust. Therefore, data for some congregations initially included in the sample were simply unavailable for inspection by the research team or, for that matter, by anyone who would find them helpful in fiscal planning for the 1980s. This was true for about one of every five congregations asked to be in the study.

Moreover, there are many differences in the ways congregations report their expenses, and categories within the treasurer's reports are not consistent from year to year. For example, one congregation reported a 400 percent increase in utility expenses one year. The increase was the result of a repair to the heating system, which was included under utility expenses. The research staff spent many hours sorting out such variances in reporting. Categories or "lines" used by church treasurers for accounting purposes change very slowly, and often treasurers "bury" expense items in reporting categories with names that do not remotely reflect the actual expenditures. But the inclusion of what would normally be thought of as a capital item in the annual operating budget is the most frequent accounting error normally discovered. Many church treasurers apparently do not distinguish between capital and current operating expenses. Some even report the proceeds of loans secured as income to the annual fund. This hides the long-range effects of inflation and contributes to poor accounting practices.

Finally, the amount of time required for the participating congregations to sort through their records and to provide the requested data for the research was longer than expected. The average amount of time from the point when the congregation agreed to participate until they had finished supplying the requisite data exceeded six months.

Notwithstanding these difficulties, the data resulting from this effort are without parallel for describing the financial characteristics of congregations. Moreover, pastors of congregations that did provide data for the study say the exercise was helpful in getting an overall picture of the church finance system. Most congregations have not studied their financial trends over time, and collecting these data made trend analysis possible for the first time, an unexpected benefit of their participation.

Consequences of Not Planning

Many churches apparently do not engage in financial planning. In failing to do so, they miss opportunities to attract new income or to realize significant savings when the results they seek can be achieved with less expensive resources. They are more vulnerable to losing track of their money, as is the case with the church called LUCK presented in Appendix I. They are even more vulnerable to theft by a trusted official who, not being watched or supported in his or her work, finds temptation irresistible.

More importantly, in addition to risking the above problems, the church with no financial planning is unable to tell its members how the money they give has been spent or what larger contributions on their part would allow the church to do. As a result the church has less income and members are deprived of the opportunity to understand their contributions to the church as being a cooperative effort to work with God, as opposed simply to giving to God (see Chapter II). To abandon making the financial decisions available to local churches is to abandon the opportunity to participate in God's creative activity. It is to ignore the church's mission and purpose.

Some Implications for Interpreting the Data

The difficulties encountered in collecting the data have placed some limitations on the project as a whole. These difficulties are raised here as cautions to the readers of this report.

Instead of having the advantage of a random selection of congregations from which to argue for the degree to which the sample is representative, the researchers had to collect data where they could be obtained and base their arguments for representativeness on comparison of the sample data to population statistics provided by denominations.

Struggling churches, small churches, and churches in the midst of financial crisis and declining membership have the poorest records. Financial records for churches that have closed during the past decade are virtually nonexistent, although sufficient information about closed churches has been obtained for the purpose of developing some of the case studies in Appendix I.

Leaders motivated to participate in this study may be more alert to financial problems in their congregations. Because of their awareness and participation, the study itself may possibly have an effect on the financial future of these congregations.

When the preliminary data were collected in spring through fall 1979, the expenditures for 1979 were unavailable. The research team has assembled the 1979 data and some 1980 data. The team found that data are most accessible for the year just completed. Future researchers would be well advised to do annual panel studies for congregational finances rather than to seek historical data.

In some instances, congregations could provide data for some but not all years requested. For these congregations, estimates were constructed based on their performance in years for which data were available. These estimates were made in such a way as to minimize any trends. As a result they fail to take into account any exceptional event of financial importance to the congregation that may have occurred during years for which data are missing.

CHAPTER VI

<hr>

How Churches Cope with Inflation and Recession

Overview

By studying how the sample congregations have fared in the recent economic environment, church leaders can have some basis on which to evaluate their own records. Also, some patterns emerge showing the decisions leaders in the sample churches have been making in order to cope with inflation and recession. As noted in Chapter III, most denominations had constant or falling real-dollar receipts during the 1970s. The churches in the sample follow this general pattern, as Table 4 shows. The average income over the years for the 75 congregations varies narrowly around $42,000, when dollars are held constant at their 1967 value. Some churches have experienced a dramatic increase in real receipts during the 1970s, while others have remained relatively stable. And, finally, the largest number have experienced a serious decline in the value of their receipts. In this chapter, the characteristics of these three types of churches will be discussed, with emphasis on patterns of income and acquisition of resources (expenditures). During the 1970s and into the 1980s there has been significant change in the proportion of the total funds congregations spend for particular goods and services. More of the church dollar is spent for resources like utilities and less for resources like benevolence and pastoral services.

Sources of Income

The congregations in the sample differ dramatically in how well they are coping with financial aspects of their existence. About a fourth of them (18 of the 75) are experiencing a real increase in spending power when the value of their total income and expense is calculated in constant dollars (1967 = 100), and 23 of the congregations (31 percent) have remained fairly stable over the past few years. Thirty-four congregations, or about 45 percent, are not keeping up with inflation. In order to determine how well church income held up to inflation, income and expense were adjusted to reflect the 1967 value of the dollar. Moreover, since income and expense were found to be erratic from year to year (because of major bequests, special fund drives, large one-time expenditures), five-year averages were developed in order to emphasize long-range trends. The final figure for determining the trend of a congregation's 1979 total income, therefore, would be the average of 1975, 1976, 1977, 1978, and 1979, expressed in terms of 1967 dollars.

The 75 congregations were divided into three economic types on the basis of their income: type 1, those reporting a gain of over 10 percent in annual cash flow (in both total income and offerings) over the past *five* years; type 2, those that have not increased or decreased more than 10 percent; and type 3, those that decreased more than 10 percent. Table

4 traces the income patterns of these congregations since 1970.

The financially growing congregations show regular increases from 1970 through 1979. Stable congregations, while showing modest gains early in the decade, maintained fairly constant incomes for the past five years. The 23 declining congregations show a marked decrease in income, finishing 1979 with an average 29.79 percent decline from 1970.

By far the largest single source of income for all three types of local churches, as expected, is the regular offering of members. In most years this accounts for between 80 and 85 percent of all income. Special gifts and bequests, the second largest source, amounted to only 7.62 percent in 1979, while income from endowment accounted for an additional 5.27 percent. Less than one percent came from direct denominational subsidies, and a similar amount was netted from fairs and bazaars. Rental of church-owned property amounted to 1.11 percent of all income in 1979.

About two-thirds (51) of the congregations reported receiving some income from endowment in 1979, while only 43 reported endowment income in 1970, an increase of over 18

TABLE 4

Average Income from All Sources,
1970–79 (1967 = 100)

Year	Growing Churches ($N = 18$)	Stable Churches ($N = 23$)	Declining Churches ($N = 34$)	Total ($N = 75$)
1970	$34,247	$36,741	$55,079	$44,455
1971	34,642	38,024	49,207	42,282
1972	35,101	39,994	48,211	42,545
1973	37,525	39,627	46,767	42,359
1974	37,842	40,832	44,823	41,924
1975	39,811	40,347	43,100	41,466
1976	42,972	39,652	42,725	41,841
1977	46,213	40,794	41,984	42,634
1978	47,547	40,621	39,744	41,886
1979	48,691	40,375	38,672	41,598

percent for the decade. In 1979, 52 congregations received gifts or bequests, while only 33 received gifts and bequests in 1970. Three churches received denominational subsidies in 1970, and seven received income in this way in 1979. More and more churches are seeking income from sources other than offerings. In the model presented in Diagram 2, decision point B (which has to do with management of sources of income other than offerings) will become of increasing importance to local church leaders.

Rural congregations have fared slightly better than their urban counterparts, perhaps because they are smaller and less affected by inflation. Rural churches also tend to have lower ratios of fixed to variable costs. Nevertheless, there is no one community type where all churches are in difficulty or free from it. When the urban category is broken further into community subcategories, it may be noted that of the three inner-city congregations in the sample, one had stable income and two had decreasing incomes. Inner-city churches are acutely affected by constituency changes. Table 5 shows the results of the community breakdown.

As might be expected, congregations with increasing membership, as shown in Table 6, have generally fared better than congregations with stable or decreasing membership (although some congregations with decreasing membership have done very well financially). Moreover, there are a few churches in which financial growth lags behind growth in membership, indicating that a growth in number of members does not necessarily insure growth in income.

Churches in the middle range of membership size, especially those between 400 and 800 members, had a more difficult time keeping up with inflation than did the small or extremely large congregations (Table 7). One plausible explanation for this is that while the largest churches can support a large building and a full program and the smaller churches have never had a full program and have no need to implement extensive programs or build large buildings, the middle-sized

103

TABLE 5
Three Economic Types of Congregation by Community Type (N = 75)

	URBAN		SUBURBAN		FRINGE AREA		RURAL SMALL TOWN		TOTAL	
	N	%	N	%	N	%	N	%	N	%
Growing	7	39	5	28	3	17	3	17	18	100
Stable	8	35	1	4	5	22	9	39	23	100
Declining	16	47	8	24	4	12	6	18	34	100
Total	31	41	14	19	12	16	18	24	75	100

TABLE 6
Three Economic Types of Congregation by Membership Growth or Decline (N = 75)

	LARGE INCREASE[a]		SMALL INCREASE[b]		SMALL DECREASE[c]		LARGE DECREASE[d]		TOTAL	
	N	%	N	%	N	%	N	%	N	%
Growing	8	44	7	39	3	17	0	0	18	100
Stable	2	9	12	52	6	26	3	13	23	100
Declining	2	6	5	15	20	59	7	21	34	100
Total	12	16	24	32	29	39	10	13	75	100

[a] Large increase = over 8 percent since 1975
[b] Small increase = 8 or less percent since 1975
[c] Small decrease = 8 or less percent since 1975
[d] Large decrease = over 8 percent since 1975

churches are more likely to have needs and/or expectations for a full program and large building but insufficient income for supporting them. Moreover, large and small churches may find it easier to change their demands for particular goods and services when they become too costly than is the case for middle-sized churches. For example, if the large church has two secretaries, it can probably reduce its staff by one secretary, whereas the middle-sized church only has one secretary. Many middle-sized churches occupy buildings almost as large and as expensive to maintain as do large-membership churches. In a small congregation, a half-time pastor may be reduced to quarter time without members perceiving that the church is in danger of closing or even in serious financial difficulty. The small church does not aspire to acquire high-cost resources in order to achieve its desired results in ministry.

Attendance at worship is the single most important factor in predicting the total amount of a congregation's income. Not surprisingly, a church with larger membership and attendance has greater income. Moreover, a congregation can reduce its number of members by removing inactive persons from the rolls without affecting either the attendance level or the amount of income from contributions. When attendance wanes, however, the financial well-being of the congregation can be expected to be in jeopardy notwithstanding redoubled efforts on the part of remaining members. The dependency of income on attendance is reasonably to be expected, since churches depend heavily on contributions for their income, and people who attend regularly contribute more frequently and in larger amounts. When the growth in attendance, 1970 to 1979, is correlated with the growth in income for the same decade, the resulting coefficient is $r = 0.55$. (Note: In the following paragraphs, the correlation coefficients reported are the correlations between the sample congregations' rates of growth 1970–79 and other selected variables. A correlation coefficient is an indicator of the degree to which the two

TABLE 7
Three Economic Types of Congregation
by Size of Membership (N = 75)

	UNDER 200		200–399		400–799		800 AND OVER		TOTAL	
	N	%	N	%	N	%	N	%	N	%
Growing	5	28	6	33	3	17	4	22	18	100
Stable	3	13	6	26	12	52	2	9	23	100
Declining	2	6	12	35	17	50	3	9	34	100
Total	10	13	24	32	32	43	9	12	75	100

variables are associated with each other. The correlation coefficient is represented by r and ranges from $+1$ to -1. A negative r indicates that as one variable increases, the other decreases.) As attendance goes up, does income tend to go up too? The answer is yes, based on the correlation coefficient of 0.55.

Can members of a church with declining attendance be motivated to give enough money to keep the church stable or growing economically? Analysis of the 1979 giving per member in the sample churches yields some insights into this question. This ratio, which may be interpreted as the amount of money contributed by the average worshiper in 1979, ranges from a low of $43 to a high of $389 in the sample churches. The median is $190. This ratio goes up significantly in churches in economic decline ($r = -0.48$). That is to say, individual members of churches in economic decline (in which total income is not keeping up with inflation) tend to give more to the church than do members of churches that are keeping up with or growing faster than the inflation rate. This suggests that when churches face financial difficulties, the active members respond by increasing their contributions. Yet for the churches in overall economic decline, the amount of this increase is insufficient to keep the churches stable or growing economically. This brings into question the practice of depending on members to increase their contributions as a long-range strategy for dealing with economic problems.

Are churches with financial guarantors—one or a few people who give much more money than the average church attender—more likely to have grown economically in the past decade than churches without such wealthy benefactors? In the sample churches, the proportion of total church income contributed by the 10 largest contributors ranges from a low of 5 percent to a high of 50 percent, and the median is 17 percent. Churches with a few very large contributors have not grown significantly faster economically or declined more rapidly during the past decade than did churches without such guarantors ($r = 0.17$).

Some congregations have large, expensive-to-maintain buildings with little income to pay for maintenance. Such churches are especially vulnerable because unexpected major maintenance could force the church to close. Prospective new members may find such churches unattractive because of the incongruity of large buildings (perhaps ill maintained), minimal programs, and the general pall created in such churches by apparent lifelessness. The ratio of the 1979 expenses to the replacement value of the church building is one indicator of the incongruity of the program with the building and of how well a congregation can withstand unexpected major maintenance. In the sample churches, this proportion ranged from 1 to 54 percent, with an average of 14.5 percent. This means that the annual total expenditures for the average church in the sample is 14.5 percent of the replacement value of the church buildings. But in some churches, there is only $1 spent per year for every $100 of replacement value of the building. While there is no general rule as to what this percentage should be, any church for which this percentage is 10 or less would be well advised to study how well it could cope with unexpected major maintenance and to study whether the building is appropriate for the program. Of the present sample, 47.3 percent fall in this category. This ratio is correlated with how well the church has done over the past decade in receiving income ($r = 0.39$). The churches doing poorly economically are more likely to have budgets that are small in comparison to their building replacement value, and the churches doing well tend to have budgets that are much larger by comparison to the replacement value. In other words, one indicator of how well a church is doing financially is to compare the replacement value of its building with its annual budget. Churches where the annual budgets are but a small fraction of the value of their buildings are more likely to be having trouble keeping up with inflation, not only because their expenses are high, but also because they have more difficulty getting income necessary for their budgets.

Are churches with endowments doing better than churches without them? Have endowments that have increased or decreased in value helped or hurt the churches in terms of total income for annual expenses? The ratio of the value of the endowment in 1979 to the value in 1975 can be correlated with economic growth to address these issues. (The year 1975 was chosen because very few churches could report values for 1970.) Of the sample churches, 25 had no endowments in either 1975 or 1979. The remainder, which had endowments both years, show ratios beginning with zero (one church spent all its endowment) and three churches increasing their endowment during this five-year period by over 1,000 percent. The median increase is 136 percent. The increase or decrease in value of the endowment contributes, in the expected way, to the annual growth of annual income to churches. Yet, increasing endowments does not guarantee the church will keep up with inflation; when growth of endowment is correlated with overall economic growth, the resulting coefficient is only $r = 0.05$. As a quick test of their own situation, church leaders may use the following proposition to assess the effects of endowments on giving through offerings. If the deflated amount of offering received per year per member goes down over a period of five years as the value of the endowment increases, endowment may be suspected of negatively affecting motivation to give. If average giving and endowment are both up, there appears to be no such negative result.

Are churches that are more dependent on their endowment for income growing faster or slower than churches that depend more on the weekly offerings? Nineteen churches in the sample report no endowments in 1979. The ratio of the value of the 1979 endowment to the 1979 income in those churches with endowments ranges from 4 percent to 554 percent, with a median of 13.5 percent. Churches with high ratios of value of endowment to annual income appear to have grown somewhat more slowly economically than churches with low ratios ($r = -0.26$). In other words, churches with larger endowments are not as likely to have grown economically as are churches with small or no endowments.

How well are churches with large numbers of retired members or large numbers of people in their early careers doing in keeping up with inflation? The proportion of retired persons in the sample congregations ranged from a low of zero percent to a high of 49 percent, with a median of 17.75 percent. The congregations with larger proportions of retired people have a somewhat more difficult time keeping up with inflation ($r = -0.21$). Consequently, alternatives to heavy dependence on weekly contributions of members need to be explored in these churches. The churches with larger proportions of people between ages 25 and 45 have done better at keeping income levels of the church growing ($r = 0.29$). One church reported only 14 percent of its membership in this age level, and one had 50 percent, the low and high of the range. The median is 27.8 percent. It may be supposed that age is related to the amount of spendable income individuals have, the retired and young-adult church members having less and persons in peak production years having more income.

The foregoing correlations may be considered as being only preliminary in nature; more research is needed to refine their implications. The results of data collected from the 75 churches, however, may be summarized as follows.

- Total income from giving is closely related to attendance at worship.
- In economically declining churches that are losing members, remaining members are often motivated to give more money per person, but this increase in the amount some people give is insufficient to offset losses.
- Churches with a few big contributors are no more or less likely to have grown economically than churches

without such financial guarantors, although churches with financial guarantors are more vulnerable to decline if these guarantors leave the church.
- Churches with low income and large buildings are especially likely to be in economic decline and may be vulnerable to closing because they are unable to pay for unexpected major maintenance.
- Churches with larger endowments appear not to have done quite as well in keeping up with inflation as those with small or no endowments.
- Churches with larger proportions of older members have had more difficulty in keeping up with inflation than have churches with larger proportions of younger and middle-aged members.

These various correlations, preliminary as they may be, do have several strategy implications for local church financial planners, which can be summarized as follows: Planners need to monitor carefully any factors related to increase or decline in worship attendance. If a decline is noted, the remaining attenders may be encouraged to contribute more money than their counterparts in other churches, but this increase will probably not be enough to keep the church from losing ground against inflation. Other measures will be necessary to generate new income if the church is to keep at par.

Middle-sized or large churches may be especially vulnerable. Unexpected major maintenance, a potential church killer, is especially dangerous to congregations of all sizes, and particularly to churches with sharply declining membership and highly valuable properties. Alternative approaches to providing space for the congregations in this situation need to be explored. Finally, churches that minister to retired persons in significant numbers need to explore alternative ways of producing income—for example, bequests and deferred giving—even though this may not insure their keeping pace with inflation.

TABLE 8

Average Total Expenditures for All Purposes, 1970–79 (1967 = 100)

Year	Growing Churches (N = 18)	Stable Churches (N = 23)	Declining Churches (N = 34)	Total (N = 75)
1970	33,842	37,017	53,722	43,827
1971	34,017	37,243	49,321	41,944
1972	34,692	37,981	48,301	41,870
1973	36,210	39,971	46,792	42,158
1974	35,423	38,044	44,937	40,539
1975	37,490	37,690	43,421	40,240
1976	42,785	36,881	42,821	40,991
1977	45,992	38,721	42,120	42,385
1978	47,569	58,542	40,860	41,759
1979	48,931	39,298	39,233	41,580

Changes in Expenditures for Resources

Table 8 shows the average amounts of expenditures for the three types of congregations—growing, stable, and declining—and for the total sample. The averages follow, with very few exceptions, the general pattern of Table 4, which reports income, because churches expend almost all their annual income in the year they receive it. Economically increasing and stable congregations characteristically receive some income in excess of expenses, while expenses are usually greater than income for economically decreasing congregations, requiring the use of any capital reserves to make up the differences.

Two approaches to analyzing expenses were followed, the first dividing the expenditures into six categories, based on whether the expense was related to the number of members or attenders in the church and whether the expense could be described as fixed, operating, or discretionary. Fixed costs are those to which the congregation is morally if not legally committed at the time the budget is determined. The second approach traces patterns of change in costs for particular re-

112

sources over the 1970 decade—for example, utilities, pastors' salaries, and so forth.

Categories of expenses. Most local church treasurers keep the financial records arranged in categories that allow the integrity of the record-keeping process to be verified through audits. A few keep records in such a way that the main results a church seeks are clearly visible. See, for example, the two budgets included in Appendix II. The categories used below represent a different approach to categorizing expenses, designed to help local church financial leaders make difficult decisions. The categories are helpful in financial planning especially at decision points *C* and *F* on Diagram 2 (page 79).

While no church will want to arrange its bookkeeping along these lines, looking at the expenses in these categories for planning purposes will give new perspectives on old fiscal problems. The budget of any church, with slight modifications, can be arranged in these categories as an analytical exercise. The categories are:

1. Expenses that increase or decrease as the number of members/attenders increases or decreases (costs of having a new member or attender).

   a. Fixed expenses: benevolences required or suggested as a fair share by the denomination.
   b. Operating expenses: consumable supplies for maintenance and other purposes, church bulletins, kitchen supplies, church publications.
   c. Discretionary expenses: educational and fellowship program costs, promotional costs.

2. Expenses that remain constant as the number of members/ attenders increases or decreases.

   a. Fixed expenses: utilities, mortgage payment or other debt reduction, insurance, essential capital improvements or renovations.

113

b. Operating expenses: salaries for pastor(s) and staff.
c. Discretionary expenses: music program, voluntary benevolence or service contribution in addition to money requested by the denomination, elective capital improvements and renovations, contributions to local governments in lieu of taxes.

The actual expenses placed in the six categories may vary from congregation to congregation. For example, music program expenses may in some instances go up as the number of members goes up; but in most instances, the cost for the music program stays the same whether 100 or 1,000 people hear the choir on a particular Sunday.

Of critical importance to financial planners are the funds expended in the two "discretionary" categories. The decisions made about these funds are those that will especially affect the life and health of the congregation. If the amount of funds for discretionary uses is low, financial planners seek to make long-term decisions to reduce fixed and operating costs. Moreover, if income drops while fixed and operating costs are high, and no discretionary money is available, the church faces economic decisions of dire consequence.

The expenses related to the number of members/attenders are somewhat self-adjusting when the church has dramatic increases or decreases in income, while the other expenses are not. As shown below, most expenses of a local church are of the nonself-adjusting variety. Therefore, increases and especially decreases in membership necessitate prompt financial decisions.

Table 9 gives percentages for each category of expense for the year 1979, plus the percent of increase or decrease for the decade 1970–79. Six observations about the data reported on this table may be made.

First, the largest part of the local church expenses is not related to the number of members. As additional members join or people leave membership, these expenses remain con-

TABLE 9

Categories of Expenses, Percentage of Increase or Decrease After Inflation Factor Is Removed, 1970–79, and Percentage of Total Expense in 1979

Expense Categories	GROWING CHURCHES		STABLE CHURCHES		DECLINING CHURCHES	
	% increase or decrease 1970–79	% of total 1979 expense	% increase or decrease 1970–79	% of total 1979 expense	% increase or decrease 1970–79	% of total 1979 expense
Member/attender related						
Fixed	65	11	− 26	10	− 32	12
Operating	− 24	5	− 24	7	− 21	8
Discretionary	− 37	3	− 7	4	− 30	3
Not member/attender related						
Fixed	69	34	41	28	− 41	19
Operating	23	37	− 3	37	− 13	44
Discretionary	1	10	16	14	− 10	14
All expense categories	45		6		− 27	

stant. For economically growing churches, these expenses amount to 81 percent of the total expense. For financially stable churches, they amount to 79 percent, and for declining churches 77 percent. Therefore, the church with growing membership can keep its expenses comparatively constant, while more people share the financial burden. When these nonmember-related expenses do need to increase, they tend to go in large leaps (e.g., the addition of a second pastor, the building of a larger sanctuary or educational unit, the addition of a new mission project). These things can be added when the growing number of members contribute sufficiently to underwrite such major additions to expenses, and they are heralded as major economic accomplishments of the church. Similarly, when the number of members declines, these costs remain stable, unless they are reduced in large amounts (e.g., final payment of mortgage, reduction in ministerial staff, decisions not to insure the buildings at replacement value, cutback in music or mission programs). When these changes occur, the church passes through those important economic thresholds listed earlier. Members may interpret changes as signs of a serious decline, which affects the general morale of the church. Pastors often identify these changes as major turning points in the economic life of congregations. An analysis of their observations is included in Chapter VII.

Second, churches that are growing economically have posted the largest increases in the area of fixed expenses, both of the member-related and nonmember-related variety. Declining churches have cut back most severely in these expenses by paying off mortgages and not incurring additional capital expense, probably at the cost of deferring major maintenance. While economically growing churches have 45 percent of their expenses falling in the two fixed-expense categories, declining churches have only 31 percent expended in this way.

Third, churches expend very little for discretionary purposes. The range is from 13 percent for growing churches to

18 percent for stable congregations. Yet the programs included under these rubrics—for example, educational programs, voluntary benevolences, music—are those that give the church its character. They are closest to reflecting the church's objectives and values. People are attracted to or repelled from churches by the quality of educational and music programs, by the way the church expends money for missions, and so forth.

Fourth, churches of all three types have made reductions in the proportion of the money they spend for operating and discretionary expenses of the member-related variety. That is to say, churches are spending less of their money on maintenance supplies, educational programs, and fellowship programs. But, because the amount of funds the church expends for these things is comparatively small, the overall change for the past decade is not very great.

Fifth, declining churches have cut back in all areas, but most severely in the areas of fixed expenses. They have been least successful in cutting back on operating costs (especially salaries). In Chapter VII, some light is shed on this result. Church financial leaders indicate what expense would be the last to be cut in the event of a financial disaster: pastors' salaries.

Sixth, in 1979 the proportion of fixed, member-related costs is about the same for all three types. This means, since the only item in this category is benevolence required by the denomination, that a dollar contributed in any of the three types of churches will result in 10 to 12 cents going to the denomination.

When specific expenses are grouped in the ways local churches more characteristically construct their budgets, the resulting picture is somewhat different, as indicated in the following.

Changing proportions of expenses. The proportion of the total expenditure for particular goods and services has

CHART 6. Proportion of Total Funds Expended for
Pastoral Services, 1970-79, in 75
Local Churches

changed in important ways during the 1970s. Chart 6 shows the proportion of the total expenditure for pastoral services from 1970 to 1979. While the total real income and expenditure for these 75 churches has stayed about the same throughout the decade, the proportion of their expenditures to purchase pastoral services has declined slightly in every year except 1975. Said another way, in 1970 a total of 34.6 cents of every dollar spent by the 75 congregations was paid to the pastor as salary, benefits, or expenses. By 1979, this had dropped to 29.2 cents per dollar expended.

As inflation increased costs of other parts of the congregations' market baskets, one way leaders coped was to cut the proportion of funds used for pastoral services. The usual way they did this was to reduce part-time staff or to move slowly in filling pastoral vacancies. In a few cases, decreasing churches went from a full-time to a part-time pastor or from two full-time pastors to one. Pastors who stayed full time tended to

118

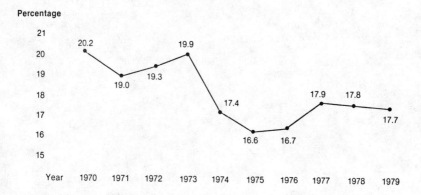

CHART 7. Proportion of Total Funds Expended for Benevolence Giving, 1970-79, in 75 Local Churches

have salaries that kept up with inflation in terms of real dollars.

Chart 7 shows a curvilinear pattern for the portion of funds expended for required and voluntary benevolences. The 75 churches averaged 20.2 cents per dollar contributed in 1970, and reached a low of 16.56 cents in 1975. Slight gains followed in the next years. The sharp decline in 1974 and 1975 coincides with the rapid inflation of those years.

By way of contrast, as shown in Chart 8, the amount paid for utilities increased sharply during the 1970s. At the beginning of this decade, only 7.3 percent of church expenditures was for utilities, but by 1979 this proportion had reached 10.9 percent. The rise is, in fact, not so sharp as the increase in fuel costs might lead one to expect. This indicates the churches have found ways of economizing, either by turning back thermostats or by retrofitting their buildings and heating plants, or both. Nevertheless, churches are paying more of their money for utilities.

Insurance costs have also gone up. In fact, some churches are paying 400 percent more for insurance in 1979 than they were in 1970, which may reflect underinsured conditions and/

119

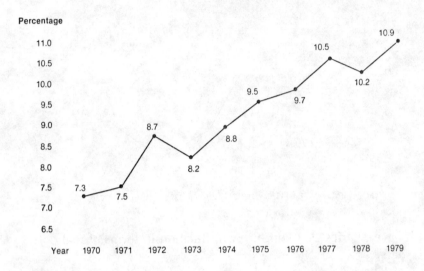

CHART 8. Proportion of Total Funds Expended for Utilities, 1970-79, in 75 Local Churches

or changes in insurance risk. Chart 9 plots the increase in insurance costs. Local churches can do very little about the broad trends in insurance rates, but they can get several bids in order to obtain the lowest rates possible. In some instances, cooperative programs sponsored by judicatories have been able to obtain the average lowest cost per church. Some churches, however, follow the questionable practice of deliberately insuring their buildings for less than their replacement cost in order to cut back on expenses. Churches with large, ornate, expensive-to-replace buildings in high-risk communities have especially high insurance rates. Unfortunately, these same churches have other very high expenses too, and often not enough income to cover costs. If the buildings are not to be insured at replacement value, the amount of insurance payment in the event of loss of the building should be sufficient to carry on some form of ministry in a new location.

The proportion of funds for educational programs (Chart 10)

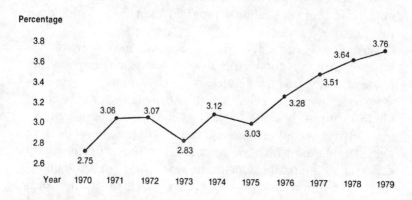

CHART 9. Proportion of Total Funds Expended for Insurance, 1970-79, in 75 Local Churches

has gone down. In fact, churches appear to spend surprisingly little for their educational programs, owing principally to the large number of volunteers (and paid staff such as pastors with salaries counted other places) who provide materials as well as instruction. This part of church expenditures is vulnerable to

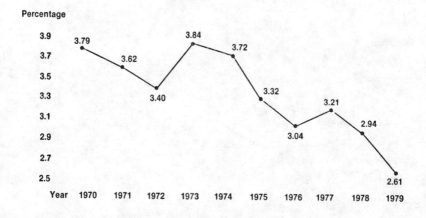

CHART 10. Proportion of Total Funds Expended for Educational Programs, 1970-79, in 75 Local Churches

121

cost-cutting measures, however, because it is something the church can control. As it is, most churches have less cash outlay for their educational program than they do for their maintenance supplies.

Costs for secretarial services (Chart 11) have increased in the proportion of total expense they represent, perhaps because costs for pastoral services have decreased. As expenses for pastors increase, relying on less expensive, paid lay help for tasks formerly done by pastors may become an increasingly attractive option. Several of the sample churches have paid secretaries who now do administrative work formerly expected of the pastor. One of the case studies in Appendix I, "A New Church for Newark," provides an illustration of a congregation for which one option would be to employ several lay persons as staff members and to seek only the part-time services of an ordained pastor.

By way of contrast, costs for maintenance staff have gone down (Chart 12). Perhaps it is easier to find people who will volunteer to do maintenance work than it is to find reliable volunteer secretaries.

CHART 11. Proportion of Total Funds Expended for Secretarial Services, 1970-79, in 75 Local Churches

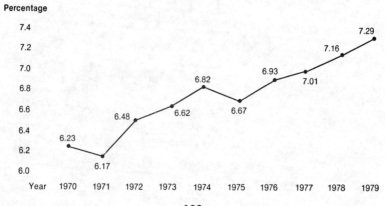

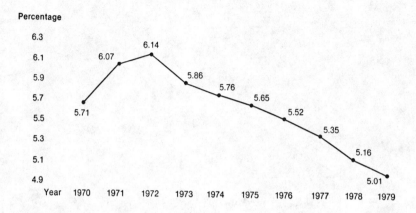

CHART 12. Proportion of Total Funds Expended for
Maintenance Staff, 1970-79, in 75
Local Churches

Maintenance supplies (Chart 13) are requiring more of the church dollar, reflecting inflation in the area of consumable products. Churches appear to be unable to cut back on these requirements significantly to blunt inflation.

The proportion of funds spent for capital improvements and debt reduction (including interest) has gone up somewhat, as shown in Chart 14, but not as much as might be expected given the great cost increases in construction. The amounts paid for capital improvements and debt reduction have gone up sharply for growing and stable churches and have decreased for churches with declining finances. This suggests that many congregations with declining finances are deferring major maintenance as a strategy for coping with inflation. The amount spent (constant dollars) for construction in religion actually went down during the decade. How long a church can defer major maintenance, or delay plans for necessary expansion, without irreparable harm is not easily determined. But it is a major policy decision faced by the financial leaders of many congregations.

The expenditures reported on Charts 6 through 14 account

123

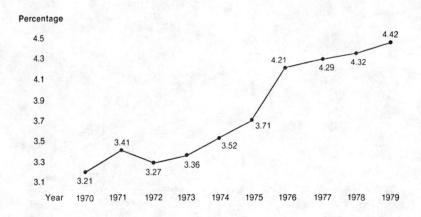

CHART 13. Proportion of Total Funds Expended for Maintenance Supplies, 1970-79, in 75 Local Churches

for roughly 95 percent of the churches' total expenditure. The remaining 5 percent may be described as incidental costs. The charts present a key to understanding how churches have coped with inflation. Some parts of their costs have increased dramatically; as a result, other parts received proportionately less of the church dollar. Charts with descending lines indicate those areas where the churches have been most successful in effecting economies in inflationary times.

Fluctuations in Income

Income and expenses do not flow from year to year in a smooth curve upward or downward for the congregations in this sample. On the contrary, they sometimes fluctuate by increases of over 100 percent and by comparable decreases of 50 percent when compared to the previous year's income. The data for this study were collected for an aggregated total of 894 years of experience in the sample churches, and in 208 of these years (23 percent) the congregations reported an increase in total income of 10 percent or more.

124

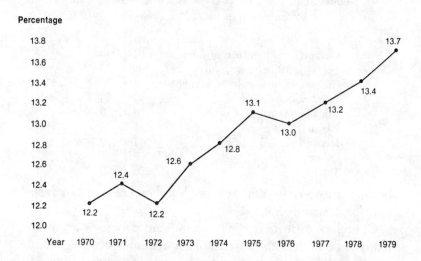

CHART 14. Proportion of Total Funds Expended for Capital Expenses (Including Debt Reduction), 1970-79, in 75 Local Churches

Percentage

13.8   13.7
13.6
13.4   13.4
13.2   13.1   13.2
13.0   13.0
12.8   12.8
12.6   12.6
12.4   12.4
12.2
12.2   12.2
12.0

Year 1970 1971 1972 1973 1974 1975 1976 1977 1978 1979

Table 10 tabulates the principal sources of increase for the years in which gains were made. Increases in regular giving and special gifts account for most of the increases, followed by fund-raising drives and increased income from investments. Other reasons for increase are infrequently given. When the increase comes from gifts and bequests, there is a similar decrease in income the following year. Increases resulting from larger regular offerings are more likely to be long-term gains that continue for several years.

Some Other Economic Processes

Thirty-four percent of the churches provide housing allowances for pastors; the remaining churches own parsonages. Housing allowances are much more common among churches with declining expenditures, about 60 percent providing the allowance. These churches may have moved to housing allowances in order to raise capital by selling the parsonages or

TABLE 10

Number of Years in Which Sample Congregations
Reported an Increase of Over 10 Percent in Income
by Category of Increase, 1965–79

	N	%
Offerings and regular contributions	81	40
Special gifts, bequests, wills	69	33
Endowments, rentals, investments	21	10
Fund-raising drives	20	10
Sale of property	7	3
Bazaars, fairs	6	3
Denominational subsidy	1	0.5
Other	3	1
Total	208	100

because they are located in a neighborhood deemed undesirable for a pastor's home.

Churches with increasing income and expenses are more likely to be in debt than are stable or declining congregations, and the total indebtedness of the financially growing churches exceeds twice the combined indebtedness of the stable and declining churches. This is because growing churches are in more need of capital investment in buildings.

Endowments are more common among churches with declining expenditures. About 53 percent of the declining churches have endowments that produced income of over $1,000 in 1979, while 33 percent of the churches with increasing expenditures have similar endowment income. Forced to rely on income other than offerings, the declining churches have been more successful in seeking bequests, a strategy growing churches might consider before decline begins.

Summary

A single strategy for dealing with the financial problems facing the 75 congregations in the sample cannot be devised. Their diverse fiscal conditions preclude any cure-all approach. While developing a series of detailed strategies is beyond the purview of this volume, some elements of appropriate strategies are presented in Chapters I and VIII.

The diversity of the churches' economic conditions includes differences in long-term trends in the congregations, differences in short-term gains and losses, differences in patterns of consumption, and differences in growth and decline of membership size. The following common patterns may, however, be concluded from the analysis in this chapter. Each pattern is related to the planning model, Diagram 2, presented in Chapter IV, page 79, in order to suggest how leaders of churches with similar patterns can begin to plan their futures.

1. The financial well-being of most congregations is closely tied to the increase or decline they experience in attendance at worship. People who attend also give. Hence, decision point A on Diagram 2 continues to be critical for local church finances, especially for growing churches. How can more people be recruited? How can members be motivated to give more? Moreover, decision point D, related to the production of desired results, is critically related to the question of why people are motivated to attend and give.

2. Congregations that have members who give more on a per-member basis generally have not fared as well economically as churches in which members give less per member. Members in declining churches are motivated to give more to help their congregations survive, but the decline usually outstrips their increases in giving. Planning at decision point A is insufficient when a church is facing decline. It is not enough to ask how more members can be enrolled and how members can be encouraged to give more. Considerations of other sources of giving (point B), contemplation of changes in the desired results (point D), and review of constituencies using the results produced by the church (point E) become more necessary for planning.

3. Congregations with many older members may face serious economic problems. The church will need to rely increasingly on income from sources other than offerings (decision point *B*), but even more importantly will need to do planning at decision point *E*. Who will use the results produced by the church? What are their expectations and needs? The church with an increasing average age of members experiences a change in constituency needs in spite of the fact that the same people are continuing to attend. Members will have different expectations of their church when they are 70 years old than they did when they were 55. When the constituency changes how it uses the church's results, all other parts of the financial operations change too.

4. Churches with expensive-to-maintain buildings and small numbers of members face possible closing. Decisions about changing a church's desired results—is the sole purpose to keep the building?—are especially difficult when emotions run high, yet decisions at point *D* on Diagram 2 spell the difference between success and failure of the church.

5. Churches in the sample have found it easiest to make budget reductions in costs that go up or down according to the number of members, and harder to make reductions in costs that are not related to the number of members or attenders (see Table 9). In considering decisions at point *C* on Diagram 2—determining what resources are needed and how they are to be budgeted—leaders can be more confident about the church meeting income requirements when a proposed increase in expenses is related to the number of members or attenders. Costs that vary according to membership or attendance vary in the same way as contributed income. If attendance is up, expenses are up. If attendance falls, so do the costs.

6. Declining churches have made big cuts in the proportion of their income they spend for capital improvements and debt reduction. Having paid most of their debts, they may be unable to borrow even if they need to do so to maintain their buildings.

7. Taken as a whole, the proportion of money that sample churches expended for pastoral services, benevolences, educational programs, and maintenance staff has declined during the past decade. This reflects a change in the kinds of resources available to churches. The proportion of money expended for utilities, insurance, secretarial services, and maintenance supplies has increased in the sample churches over the past decade. With the possible exception of secretarial services, the increased cost does not mean the churches are using more of these resources. In fact, the church may be using less oil, gas, or electricity, but paying more for it. These churches have coped with inflation, it may therefore be concluded, by purchasing fewer resources when their income has not kept pace.

CHAPTER VII

Opinions of Congregation Leaders

Description of Respondents

The key element of the economic processes in the life of a local church is the people who make the financial decisions listed on Diagram 2, page 79. Leaders who make policy decisions about their congregations' financial affairs were asked to respond to some attitudinal questions regarding their perceptions of their churches' financial situations. Four hundred forty leaders from the 75 sample congregations responded.

Men outnumber women by more than two to one, with 309 men (70.3 percent) and 131 women (29.7 percent) completing the questionnaires. Their average age is 47.4 years. Just under 40 percent of the respondents hold professional positions, about 17 percent are managers or owners of businesses,

130

and just under 20 percent are clerical or sales workers. The remaining 23 percent are widely distributed through other occupations.

Almost all the respondents—432, or 98 percent—are members of one of the sample congregations. The remaining eight are part-time staff members who have financial responsibilities to the church, but happen to hold church membership elsewhere.

Most respondents have been members of the congregations for several years, with half joining before 1959 and three-quarters joining in 1970 or before. They are, moreover, frequent attenders at church, with 87.5 percent saying they are at church services every week. On the average, they spend three to four hours per week in church-related activities, and about two-thirds contribute $10 per week or more to the church.

Seventy-seven percent of the respondents have more than a high-school education, and 30 percent have more than a college education.

Two hundred thirty-seven respondents (53.9 percent) serve on finance committees; 140 serve on general governing boards that handle financial policy. Sixty-three persons (14.3 percent) indicated no formal committee membership.

Clearly, the financial policy makers and managers of church funds do not constitute a representative cross-section of the congregations. They are more highly educated, work in more prestigious occupations, are more active in church affairs, and contribute more money than average church members. Moreover, men are proportionately overrepresented.

Financial Crises and Windfalls

As noted earlier, the amount of income and expenditure sometimes varies greatly in a single congregation from year to year. Respondents were asked what would be eliminated if they had to cut expenditures and what would be done with a large unexpected sum of money if they were to receive it. In other words, what decisions would they make at point C on Diagram 2, p. 79?

Table 11 shows the ranking respondents gave to seven proposed cuts. They ranked each item, using 1 for the area where cuts would most likely be made first and 7 for the area where cuts would be made last. Benevolences clearly would be the first expenditure to be reduced, in the opinion of these respondents. Debt-reduction payments and pastors' salaries are considered to be fixed commitments or necessary operating expenses, which would be the last to be cut in an acute financial crisis.

Respondents were also asked to rank on a scale from one to four how likely their church would be to use an undesignated special gift of $50,000 in each of eight ways. Would they acquire new resources for new ministries, increase resources for present ministries, or invest the money in savings to produce future income? For each statement given in Table 12 the respondent circled a number—1 indicated "definitely," 2 indicated "very likely," 3 indicated "somewhat likely," and 4 indicated "not likely." Endowment and special programs to benefit members of the local church ranked highest, and expending the funds for current expenses ranked lowest, sur-

TABLE 11
Rank of Proposed Expenditure Cuts ($N = 440$),
Scale of 1 to 7, Most to Least

Rank Order	Mean Rank	Item
1	2.102	Church support for projects beyond the local church
2	2.827	Money sent to the denomination
3	3.672	Maintenance of church buildings
4	3.987	Educational programs
5	4.032	Staff salary, other than pastor
6	4.237	Debt-reduction payments
7	5.691	Pastor's salary

TABLE 12
Rank of Proposed Uses of a Hypothetical Gift of $50,000
(N = 440), Scale of 1 to 4, Most Likely to Least Likely

Rank Order	Mean Rank	Item
1	2.283	Place funds in endowment
2	2.321	Use for special local programs
3	2.541	Use to reduce debt
4	2.721	Purchase special equipment
5	2.842	Use for special maintenance or renovation
6	3.121	Invest money and give interest away
7	3.327	Give interest and principal to a worthy cause
8	3.811	Use for current expenses

passing even giving the money away outright, which ranked next to last.

Some Opinions About the Future

The respondents are generally optimistic about the future financial conditions of their congregations. In fact, 37.4 percent say the church will improve its financial situation, 51.8 percent predict it will stay about the same, and only 10.8 percent expect a decline. These opinions contrast starkly with the trends reported in Chapter VI. The principal factors identified by respondents as having effects on their congregations' financial future are inflation, how much people like the pastor, and changes in the number of members. While the leaders' estimates about how well their churches are or will be doing economically in the future are not supported by the data actually collected from their churches, their identification of those factors that contribute to income growth and decline is supported in part by the research data, namely, growth or decline in attendance. While they know what might happen to their churches financially, they have not analyzed their situations systematically to see if it is actually happening, nor have they engaged in realistic planning.

Opinions About Fund Raising

Each leader was asked to evaluate the acceptability of several approaches to raising funds for the congregation. Considered acceptable are mailed requests for support, special worship services to emphasize stewardship, and every-member visits to solicit funds. Fund-raising events and bazaars are acceptable, but looked upon with less favor than standard stewardship procedures. The use of outside fund-raisers and the use of bingo or other such games is generally not acceptable, as is having no formal stewardship program.

These leaders expect pastors generally to be actively involved in seeking funds for the congregation, but to share the leadership with lay people. Table 13 displays the results of a question regarding the appropriate level of involvement of pastors.

Some Conclusions About Church Financial Leaders

The opinion questionnaire provides data for four conclusions.

TABLE 13
Percentage of Responses to the Question
"How much involved in seeking funds for the church
should the pastor(s) be?" (N = 440)

%	
14.0	Highly active, vocally involved
44.6	Moderately active, somewhat vocally involved
34.6	Somewhat active, leaving most leadership to lay people
5.7	Active behind the scenes only
1.2	Completely inactive

First, the financial leaders are optimistic about their churches' economic future, although they are unaware of the effects inflation is having on their congregations (or their faith in the future notwithstanding these trends). It may be, moreover, that small increases in inflated dollar contributions and the ups and downs of year-to-year income disguise the long-term effects of inflation, and, as a result, these leaders are unaware of the reality of the decline their own congregations are experiencing.

Second, financial leaders are not demographically representative of their congregations, but are selected because of their expertise and/or prestige for these particular leadership positions. They form a kind of elite in the congregations, which can exert significant power. Church financial leaders need to be closely in touch with the goals of members for the congregation, because the formal and informal decisions financial leaders make will change the results a church actually produces and even affect the survival chances of congregations.

Third, leaders anticipate the future financial health of the congregation to be heavily dependent on the financial contributions of members. Therefore, they are likely to make decisions that will maximize income from contributions rather than to seek alternative sources of income or to make decisions that require less income without undercutting desired results.

Fourth, financial leaders place as their first priority the programs of the local church and as the lowest priority benevolence to the denomination and/or other service projects. One possible reason for low priority being given to benevolence to the denomination may be that these leaders do not perceive the benefit of these expenditures to their local churches' desired results. What the local church gets in return for the money it sends to the denomination may need to be interpreted in a cost/benefit analysis provided by the denominations.

Some Economic Transitions Noted by Pastors

Head pastors in each of the sample congregations were asked to respond to the following question: "What do you consider to be the important changes the church has experienced in the last 15 years? Include both points of growth and decline, as well as major economic decisions. Describe each briefly." Their responses fall into five main categories: events related to the churches' environmental niches, changes in membership constituencies, changes in patterns of fixed expenses that represent major economic thresholds, changes in pastoral staffing, and changes in church programs.

Changes in the churches' environmental niches have to do mainly with socioeconomic and/or ethnic changes in the neighborhood. One pastor writes, "Our members moved away and their children don't attend here anymore." Another notes, "We're now a commuter church, whereas we were a community church. We've not attracted the blacks." Still another notes that the influx of Amish and Mennonite families in the area has replaced the traditional Presbyterian constituency. A fourth observes that former city dwellers do not find the traditional approaches of the rural congregation to their liking. Urban renewal, new housing developments, factory openings and closings, and changes in ethnicity were all identified as having economic import for the churches because of the effects these have in the number of attending and contributing members.

The changes in the environment of the churches' communities results in changed constituencies of membership, the pastors observed. Changes in constituencies of membership in turn mean changes in income to the church, because the newcomers frequently provide less income than the people who have left. But other demographic changes with economic consequences were also noted by the pastors. "The number of our members over 60 years of age has greatly increased," noted one pastor, and several others reported similar trends. Another observed, "Changes in our program to emphasize social ministries have attracted several new members." Still another wrote, "Opening our doors to community programs has resulted in growth. We now have day care, a senior citizens center, a center for women, a discotheque, a missions mart, a drama group, a concert series, drug rehabilitation, and so forth."

Changes in fixed expenses (new buildings, paying off the mortgage, increased utilities, unexpected major maintenance, and the like) were most often mentioned by pastors. Where the change involved a new venture, the pastor usually viewed it positively. One pastor observed, however, that his church could not pay the debt on its $3 million building and would probably sell it. When the expense was for unexpected major maintenance, the effect was more often viewed negatively. Such expenses include the installation of Plexiglas coverings to stained-glass windows to prevent breakage, replacement of the heating plant, replacement of the organ, structural changes to stop the church tower from sinking, redecoration after deteriorated plumbing burst and ruined the fellowship-hall plaster, and repair of the church foundation because of termite damage.

Changes in pastoral staffing and the previous pastor's popularity, or lack of it, is seen by many of the pastors as having important economic implications for the churches. This reflects the opinions of lay people discussed earlier in this chapter. The pastor's personality is interpreted as being an important factor in attracting or repelling members. But, because of the subjectivity of any assessment of the pastor's personality, the level of dependence of the church's economic health on such assessment is at best conjectural. Some pastors in declining churches report they feel they have become scapegoats.

Finally, the pastors observe that changes in church programs have economic consequences. One reports, "We no longer have a youth choir." Another said, "We've stopped all evening programming for adults because people are afraid to come into the neighborhood after dark." Others report increases in membership resulting from expanded programming.

All these changes occur with regularity in churches. Planning is necessary to respond to them so that desired new results are quickly identified and supported financially.

CHAPTER VIII

Data for Financial Planning

Often local congregations do not have the data they need to make their financial decisions or do not have the data in a format that can be clearly interpreted to the average church member. This is well illustrated in the accompanying case studies (Appendix I). Most church treasurers and accountants keep records designed only for the purpose of documenting the fiscal integrity of church operations. They count offerings and report that the money has been spent for intended purposes. Such data, as essential as they are, do not exhaust the churches' need for the kind of planning advocated in Diagram 2, p. 79. This chapter provides some suggestions about how local churches can readily obtain some data for planning. The much more formidable task of setting up a system of local church accounting and financial record keeping is addressed at length in a book by Manfred Holck Jr. and Manfred Holck Sr., *Complete Handbook of Church Accounting*. The many congregations that have less-than-adequate accounting systems should consult this source or accountants who are knowledgeable about local church finances.

This chapter deals with data for planning purposes rather than data for accounting purposes. While the two objectives are similar, they differ in that planning data are wider in scope and not as detailed as accounting data. Accounting data comprise a subset of planning data. All the data church leaders find useful in making the kinds of decisions listed on Diagram 2, comprise planning data. The 10 principles governing planning data listed below, which are informed by the work of James Coleman, a sociologist and frequent policy-research consultant for the government, can guide church leaders in amassing data for planning.

1. Partial information available at the time a decision is made is better than complete information later.
2. Scope is more important than absolute accuracy of the data. Correctness of predicted results is what is important.
3. Redundancy is valuable. If several sources of data lead to the same conclusion, decision makers can be more certain about the choice they make.
4. Data that are outside the control of the congregation, such as changes in the communities and changes in denominational priorities, and generally any changes in the demographic niche, are as important to financial planning as are internal data.
5. The end results of collecting data for planning should be better decisions, not the accumulation of interesting or elaborate information.
6. Data do not make decisions. People do that, informed by their values as well as by the data.
7. Planning data need to be presented in nontechnical ways, not burdened by the technical language of finance, academics, or theology.
8. All data used to inform decisions need to be made public to the whole congregation; they should not remain in the private circles of decision makers, to

be selectively released only when it supports the decision reached.

9. When conflicting strategies are being debated, data can be independently amassed for each strategy and presented in an adversary or dialectical process.

10. Persons who present planning data can appropriately be advocates of a particular decision or strategy, but their advocacy should not affect the accuracy or thoroughness of their presentation.

These 10 principles can guide church leaders in collecting data after decisions about what questions to ask have been made. Deciding what questions to ask is a critical prior step in planning. Often churches in financial difficulty are not asking the right questions about themselves and their environment. Outside consultants are sometimes helpful by simply helping church leaders ask different questions about their situation than they are presently asking. Leaders in churches facing similar financial circumstances may, by answering different questions, arrive at very different courses of action. One may ask, "Where can we cut expenses without weakening the church program?" while another wonders, "How can we increase contributions?" A third might choose to reevaluate the desirability of the church's results. Which of these questions is right in the sense that it will lead to the discovery of the best course of action for a particular church at a particular time? The remainder of this chapter is designed to help leaders decide what kinds of decisions and what kind of data are most appropriate to their situations.

A. Contributed Income
1. Main Questions
   Can present contributors be expected under any circumstances to give more? Can the number of contributors be expected to increase?
2. Some Helpful Information
   a. Calculate the average contribution per member in the

local church compared with the denominational average (see Table 2).

b. Compute the deflated value of the total income of the church by multiplying the annual income by the decimals provided in Table 16, page 148.

c. Identify the percent of gain or loss of members/attendance over the past five years.

d. Calculate the percent of members living within a five-mile radius of the church. (If this percentage is low, members may be moving away from the church, and people moving into their former residences are not joining the church.)

e. Study the population growth in the area around the church. Use zip-code data, one to four census tract areas, or a three- to five-mile radius of the church, depending on which data are easily available. Do not use larger areas, even though some of the present members live well beyond these limits. Compare the percentage of growth in membership to that of population growth for the past five years. Project membership growth (or decline) based on how the population grows (or declines).

f. Estimate the income potential for present and prospective members. For comparison, use data on income for the same aggregated areas as listed in "d" above. These data are usually available from planning offices or through libraries.

3. Some Possible Strategies

a. If the data indicate people might be expected to give more money, strategies to improve stewardship need to be considered.

b. If the data indicate more people might be recruited to join the church, the leaders need to plan strategies to attract new members.

c. If increases are not likely either in the amounts of money people contribute or in the number of people who contribute, other strategies, such as those listed below, must be considered.

142

B. Other Income
1. Main Questions
Can income from other sources (endowment, rentals, money-raising projects, denominational subsidies) be increased by changing the way these sources are managed? Can income be increased by obtaining new capital donations or money for special programs (bequests, annuity programs for members, special program grants from businesses or denominational agencies)? Can the church liquidate some assets to be reinvested to increase income or to pay directly for some part of the church's present program of desired results?
2. Some Helpful Information
a. Identify the church's present investments (including savings accounts). Compare the rate of return on these with other possible investments.
b. List all properties, besides the church building itself, that are owned by the church. Obtain appraisals of the value of each. Identify possible future uses of each property (programs, capital gains, income production).
c. Compile a list of names of persons who have included the church in their wills.
d. Collect denominational literature on how to manage a program of wills and bequests. (The development officers in colleges and universities also have information that will be helpful.)
e. Develop a list of persons and groups outside the church's membership who might provide income to support the church (e.g., businesses that benefit from the church's presence or program, denominational agencies that have their purposes fulfilled by some aspect of the church's program, persons whose family members are buried in the church's cemetery).
f. Count the number of hours contributed by volunteers for a specific fund-raising event (bazaar, fair, etc.). Then divide the net profit of the event by the number of hours contributed. If the earnings for a volunteered

143

TABLE 14
Planning Sheet 1: Ministries and Expenses

List the important ministries offered by your congregation or other regular expenses (worship, counseling, education, community service, mission activities, debt reduction, building maintenance, utilities, etc.). Be as specific as possible in naming each.

Name of Ministry or Expense	Column 1	Column 2	Column 3	Column 4
1)		$		
2)				
3)				
4)				
5)				
6)				
7)				
8)				
9)				
10)				

In Column 1, rank the congregation's opinion of the importance this ministry has, with the number 1 being the highest in importance.

In Column 2, estimate the present cost of this ministry, including budgeted direct costs, costs of staff time, costs of facilities, etc.

Over the past 10 years, has there been any major increase or decrease in expenditures for any of these ministries? In Column 3, put a plus sign (+) or minus sign (−) for major increases and decreases. Make notes in the margins about how (on what basis) the decisions were made, or if inflation has had a big effect.

In the event of a financial "crunch" in your congregation, which ministries in your opinion would remain untouched, which would be reduced or dropped? In Column 4, put "U" for untouched, "R" for reduced, and "D" for dropped. Make marginal notes of reasons for your decisions.

On a separate page, list the expected result of each item listed and how the results relate to the congregation's overall purpose.

hour are less than the minimum wage, the event is questionable on a solely economic basis.

   3. Some Possible Strategies

      a. Reinvest the church's assets in a way that will conform to the church's financial requirements.

      b. Develop a program to recruit additional income from new sources.

      c. Implement better management policies for the church's assets.

C. Acquisition of Resources and Budget Construction

   1. Main Questions

What resources are required to accomplish the church's desired results, and what are their costs? What is the probable income to the church from each income source? What costs are fixed even before the budget process is started, which ones can be set at the time the budget is constructed, and which will be discretionary during the budget year?

   2. Some Helpful Information

      a. Planning Sheets 1 and 2 (Tables 14 and 15) provide forms on which leaders can name and evaluate ministries and leaders can categorize budget items as long-term fixed costs, costs fixed by the budget, or discretionary funds.

      b. List each desired result and the resources necessary to accomplish it. (This may require an estimate of how the pastor's time will be distributed over general ministries.)

      c. Chart the flow of income per month over the past five years to identify any cash-flow problems.

      d. Categorize expenses in general groupings such as the following: pastoral services, benevolences paid to the denomination, mission or service funds other than those paid through the denomination, costs for maintaining the building(s) including insurance and maintenance staff, office and secretarial expenses, costs of educational programs, worship expenses including music, fellowship program costs, and capital expenses such as debt reduction and any major maintenance

146

TABLE 15

Planning Sheet 2: Determination of Fixed
and Discretionary Costs

What items in your church's annual budget are *fixed costs* before the budget is ever drawn up? What items become fixed when the budget is approved? What items are discretionary during the budget year?

Fixed before the budget	Fixed by the budget	Discretionary
1)_____	1)_____	1)_____
2)_____	2)_____	2)_____
3)_____	3)_____	3)_____
4)_____	4)_____	4)_____
5)_____	5)_____	5)_____
6)_____	6)_____	6)_____
7)_____	7)_____	7)_____

paid out of current operating funds. (See, for example, the budget of Otterbein Church in Appendix II.)

e. Identify and list all new development and major maintenance projects (new construction, exterior refurbishing, organ replacement, heating plant replacement, etc.). Include the date of the last maintenance and an estimated date for future maintenance or new construction. Obtain estimates of costs for all major maintenance that could be required in the near future. Explore alternative ways for financing the new development or major maintenance (bonds sold to members, bank financing, denominational financing, bonds sold to the public, etc.). Obtain information on different kinds of loans: construction loans, mortgages, second mortgages, commercial loans, installment loans, improvement loans, and so forth.

f. Estimate the possible increases in cost if the maintenance or new construction is deferred. What other problems will develop if the maintenance is deferred? How will increased building costs limit the desired new construction if it is postponed?

g. Compare audits and treasurer's reports for the last five years to note growth or decline in specific costs.

3. Some Possible Strategies

a. Develop a budget that shows how the expenses provide resources for the desired results of the church.

b. Defend the church budget in terms of the church's priorities, not on the basis of an across-the-board percentage increase or decrease.

c. Choose a plan for financing major new construction or maintenance.

d. Develop a strategy to match expenses to the flow of income so that most expenses are to be paid when the church's income is greatest. If investment income is

TABLE 16
Purchasing Power of the Dollar, 1960–82,
with $1 Equaling 1967 Value

Year	Purchasing Power	Year	Purchasing Power
1960	$1.127	1972	$0.799
1961	1.116	1973	.752
1962	1.104	1974	.678
1963	1.091	1975	.621
1964	1.076	1976	.587
1965	1.058	1977	.551
1966	1.029	1978	.512
1967	1.000	1979	.461
1968	.960	1980	.406
1969	.911	1981	.367
1970	.860	1982	.348
1971	.824		

SOURCE: U.S. Bureau of Labor Statistics

used to subsidize current programs, income from investments can be collected in months when offerings are low.
  e. Pursue strategies that cut costs without negatively affecting the church's desired results.
D. Desired Results
  1. Main Questions
     What results does the church want to accomplish? If income is in excess of the expense for present desired results, what new results does the church want to accomplish? If income is insufficient to provide necessary resources for present desired results, which results will be left unaccomplished? How does the church define the activities and programs on which income is expanded?
  2. Some Helpful Information
     a. Draw up statements of the goals and purposes of the congregation.
     b. Prepare summaries of what program leaders are trying to accomplish through such expenses as the mission budget, educational budget, worship budget, and so on.
     c. Compile surveys of the membership's priorities for the congregation.
     d. Formulate theological interpretations of the challenges facing the church, given its location, membership, resources, and history.
  3. Some Possible Strategies
     a. Modify expenses to match as nearly as possible the realistic needs for resources to achieve desired results.
     b. Identify the results that will generate enthusiasm among present members and attract new members.
E. The Use of Results and Evaluation
  1. Main Questions
     Who benefits from the results produced by the church? What is happening to this constituency? Is their number growing or declining? Is their need increasing or declining? How is it changing? How can the church encourage accurate assessing of outcomes?
  2. Some Helpful Information

a. Examine the growth or decline of particular constituencies (age, ethnic, income, and marital-status groups) in the church and its neighborhood. Compare data for the past 10 years.

b. Collect information about how money given by the church to the denomination is used to accomplish both general and specific objectives of the congregation. What are the results of the church's expenditures in these areas? What are the dimensions of future needs?

c. Develop systematic ways of collecting constituents' opinions about church programs. Ask leaders to write down evaluative comments they hear. Use survey forms to evaluate current and possible future results of the church's activity.

d. Identify constituencies that are not presently served by the church, but could be—especially categories of people living near the church building. List the kind of opportunities the church offers these people and the kinds of resources these people would bring to the church.

3. Some Possible Strategies

a. By anticipating the future needs of present constituencies, the shape of desired future results can be projected.

b. New constituents and their needs and resources can be identified and the church's desired results modified accordingly.

F. Changes and Modifications

1. Main Questions

At what points in the overall financial system of the congregation will changes be introduced? What will the changes be?

2. Some Helpful Information

a. All the data amassed for the questions above.

b. Information about how to introduce changes.

c. Information about conflict management.

d. Audits and treasurer's reports to determine if funds have been spent as anticipated.

3. Some Possible Strategies
   a. Select the decision points where the church can make changes to improve its financial operations.
   b. Negotiate what changes need to be introduced.
   c. Manage any resulting conflict in a way that is helpful to individuals and the church as a whole.

No church is likely to want, be able, or need to collect all the data or follow all the strategies suggested in this chapter. The suggestions are intended to cover a wide range of situations and circumstances a given local church might face. Leaders, therefore, are encouraged to be selective.

The case studies that follow in Appendix I allow the reader and study groups the opportunity to apply the financial planning strategies identified in this chapter and throughout the book to specific congregations. Although the cases may be very different from the reader's own church, they can be used to apply the planning information suggested in this chapter to a variety of situations.

Case Studies

Case materials may be used by local church leaders in several ways. On the simplest level, the six cases that follow further illustrate the economic problems local churches regularly experience and the strategies they choose to cope with them. (The names of churches and persons have been changed.) Moreover, the degree to which financial considerations intertwine with the whole of church life is further documented. Beyond their illustrative value, the cases can provide church leaders comparisons and contrasts to their own situation, with the understanding that these six local churches do not necessarily provide models that should be imitated. In fact, the readers may conclude that some of the six have handled their financial affairs poorly. Comparisons will help the leaders describe their own financial problems more clearly and to discover more effective ways of tackling them.

Most important, study of the cases will help the local church financial leader increase analytical skills by identifying the problems of another church, which are ordinarily more difficult to see when they exist in one's own church. People are frequently disinclined to be candid in their assessments of themselves, yet church leaders need such candor if they are to understand their financial circumstances and to act on the variety of strategies open to them. Group study and discussion of the cases can serve as training for local church financial leaders, especially for those whose competence in matters economic lies in arenas other than church finances. The questions listed below may be used as guidelines for analyzing all the cases and for group discussion about them.

1. What are the case church's main financial problems?
2. What factors have led to these problems (change of constituency, poor planning, poor motivation for giving, mismanagement, etc.)?
3. Using Diagram 2, page 79, decide which decision points are likely to be the best for addressing the problems. For each case, there are some suggestions about which decision points may be most relevant, but these should not limit group consideration of other options.

   Specifically, consider each of the following:
   a. Can the church motivate members to give more or increase the number of members?
   b. Can the church be expected to obtain gifts and bequests? Can it increase income by managing its assets differently?
   c. Can the church improve its budget-making process? Can it substitute less expensive resources for present expensive resources? Can some costs be deferred?
   d. Can the church's goals be modified? Will the results it expects change?
   e. What changes is the church experiencing in its constituency? How are the expectations present members have of the church changing? How might prospective members evaluate the church differently than present members?
   f. At what points can changes be introduced with reasonable expectation of making improvements in the church's financial situation?

4. What additional information, other than what is provided in the case itself, would be needed in order to advise this church? How would these additional data help in making decisions? What would be the cost in time and money of obtaining these additional data? What would be the cost of delaying the decision until the additional data were available, assuming the church has no further information than what is presently reported in the case?
5. Based on the information in the case report, what courses of action would be advisable?

Some discussion questions related to each case are included at the conclusion of each case.

ST. JOHN'S OF METROPOLIS

An Overview of the Case

Even when a church closes, or is about to close, there are still decisions of economic import to be made. What is to be done with the assets of the closing congregation? Are there some pieces of property (records, artifacts) that need to be preserved because of their historical or aesthetic value? What influence, if any, does the disbanding congregation have in regard to where the remaining members transfer their membership? What is to be done about old and infirm members who are counting on the church for pastoral care and funeral rites? St. John's is one church facing such questions.

Up until their church actually closed, the members of St. John's understood the desired result of their ministry to be largely the preservation of the past. Unfortunately, this past was valued only by long-term members of St. John's Church and was becoming important to fewer and fewer people. Potential new constituents, the ethnically varied people moving into the neighborhood, did not share in St. John's past and could not be motivated to help in its preservation. In fact, St. John's members saw the inclusion of these new persons as a threat to the memory of their past. The worship liturgy served as the cement that held the remaining members together, while the other programs dropped away one by one. The Sunday school had ceased to be important to some members. Expenses were cut as far as possible, and all maintenance on the building, except for janitorial services and expenses for security, was deferred.

If St. John's were to survive as a shrine, it would have required major funding, the most likely sources being from the wills and bequests of present members. Yet, none of the older members had been encouraged to leave their estates to the church. There was some hope that former members would return in sufficient numbers to provide major support, but this proved unrealistic. Many former members had left St. John's with feelings of alienation or anger, which had in part justified their departure. Returning, to them, would mean a loss of face. St. John's had both inadequate resources and growing expenses, to which was added unimaginative and unrealistic management—a lethal combination.

The church had in fact ceased to manage its own financial affairs. The finances were managed by the emergence of crisis after crisis, such as an inadequate pastor and the failure of the heating plant. Every crisis, even the transfer of a single member out of the church, threatened the church's existence. The congregation survived as long as it could by perpetuating the memory of its past, then finally died. If the church had reached out to the community with ministries that met the needs of the new people, which perhaps would have been possible a decade before St. John's closing, then the church might have survived, but at the expense of losing what it considered its particular ministry and key desired result, preserving the value of its past. (See Tables A-1 and A-2 for statistical data.)

Using the list of major decision points of Diagram 2, page 79, St. John's situation may be described in summary as follows.

A. Membership interested in the present desired results is probably at its maximum number; members are giving at a rate much higher than their denominational average.

B. There are some older members who could provide major bequests for the church in their wills, but this practice has not been cultivated, and no one knows if the church is included in any will.

C. The church has too few resources to meet the expenses required by its desired results. It cannot afford to pay a pastor to do the liturgy and to provide pastoral care to the elderly and infirm, while maintaining the building and preserving it as a shrine to the past.

D. The congregation's main desired result is preserving the past by maintaining the building and the liturgy, as reflected by the fact that costs for security equipment and worship services come before program costs.

E. The neighborhood has changed ethnically. Present members evaluate the church's program in light of the present desired results. New people in the community are either ambivalent or hostile toward St. John's.

F. Leaders are unclear about which, if any, changes they might make will improve their situation.

The Case of St. John's

"This year the Sunday school will again sponsor the Christmas-card exchange. Please bring all the Christmas cards you plan to send to church members, and the Sunday school will deliver them for you. The money you would have used for stamps will be placed in the Sunday school treasury." Paul DeVeries, the Sunday-school superintendent, had made the same announcement for many years.

"That's pathetic," thought Mary Ellen Maxwell, whose husband is chairman of the church board. "The Sunday school was dead years ago. All that's left is Paul and his wife, Evelyn, and the new pastor's three kids."

There was a time when St. John's Sunday school had many people, more than 200. But that was before property values in the community went downhill and the Appalachian mountain people started moving in. They never fit well at St. John's; they did not like the liturgy and were not careful about the building. There were so many of them, several families crowding into homes which were built for one family. None of them ventured into St. John's Church. Now, on a good Sunday maybe 80 people would come to worship, all of them old-time members. And no one except Paul and Evelyn came to Sunday school, except on special holidays. Most people drove over 15 miles to worship at St. John's, although they or their parents had lived nearby until after World War II. The children of these older members could not even buy houses in the church's neighborhood, so they moved to the suburbs, and then to even more distant suburbs. The streets around the church were becoming run down. The houses looked so bad that blacks, aspiring to upward mobility, were not attracted to buy them. But Appalachian poor people did come, and then Hispanics and Lebanese.

Alienation between the church members and the community residents grew. Windows were broken; Plexiglas storm windows were installed to protect the stained glass. Someone broke in and pilfered the offering boxes; an elaborate burglar alarm system was installed, and all the windows were electronically wired to prevent entry. Someone climbed onto the church roof and stole the outside speaker of the burglar alarm, the only thing that would not set off the alarm. Evening meetings were canceled because members feared being mugged.

St. John's uses a historic liturgy for its worship and has an ornate sanctuary with liturgical symbols. It has a large but ailing Mohler organ. The liturgy and the beautiful sanctuary have sustained St. John's perhaps more than anything else during all its difficulties. They symbolize what is of central importance to the members.

The previous pastor had been fired after serving less than a year. The members never understood why he had so many problems, but they knew the church would die if they did not get rid of him. He spoke so softly no one could hear him preach. No one trusted him as a counselor. He would not talk to people at meetings or visit the sick. People were offended and were leaving the church. Besides, St. John's barely had enough income to keep the church building in shape, let alone to pay the salary of an ineffective pastor. "Maybe," Jerry Williams had convinced the members, "this pastor will work out. We've been looking for 14 months, and he's our only serious candidate." But he didn't work out, and everyone including Jerry was glad to see him go.

Now, an interim pastor had arrived, a professor on sabbatical leave. In exchange for living in the parsonage with his family, he would conduct worship services and visit the sick during the year he was studying at the university. Maybe, the leaders thought, we can save enough money this year to afford a pastor after he leaves. Maybe attendance will pick up now. Maybe people will want to come back.

By mid-fall, it was apparent to all that not enough people were coming back, apparent to all except those who lived in Paul DeVeries' dream world of the past. The faithful loved St. John's Church. It was the church their grandfathers and great-grandfathers built. As John Lloyd, the oldest surviving member, said, "My name's written on every brick in this building."

Memories were enshrined everywhere, even memories of memories. The professor-pastor removed the American flag from the altar so the Boy Scouts could present the colors on Scout Sunday, only to be severely scolded by Olivia Hess, a long-time member on the church board. "That flag was put there by Mrs. Whitested as a memorial to her son who died in World War II," said Olivia. "And she wanted it to stay there!" Mrs. Whitested was dead, and none of her family had been to St. John's in the past five years.

The interim pastor knew some critical decisions needed to be made, but because of his short tenure, he tried not to make them for the members. Instead, he directed his energies toward being pastoral to the members while they made their own decisions. For example, when the 60th anniversary of Henry Dixon's singing in the choir came up, the pastor suggested rededicating the organ in Henry's honor. Everyone was delighted with the idea except Olivia, who demurred because Henry had not grown up in the church; he had married a member.

Before very long, several strategies were being considered. Paul DeVeries wanted the church officially to approach St. Luke's Church, a very similar congregation about two miles away that had recently decided to close its doors. Some of its members might join St. John's, especially the soprano soloist, who had been the backbone of St. Luke's music program. With more members, St. John's would have enough money to go on.

Olivia suggested that the church write to all the previous members and their descendants to ask if they would send money to keep St. John's alive as a kind of shrine.

Both these ideas quickly proved to be unrealistic, as did Henry Dixon's. He had lived in the neighborhood of the church for 78 years. "Why," he wondered, "don't the folk move back here?"

Only four courses of action were considered by the leaders. The options took shape slowly through much informal discussion and through formal proposals at the church board meetings. By early spring, everyone knew decisions had to be made, because the interim pastor would leave the coming July. The four options can be understood better in light of the following facts, which represent the best data the leaders had in March 1975 on which to base their decisions.

FACTS ABOUT ST. JOHN'S

1. Long ago the members decided they could not reach out to new community residents who were ethnically different. Notwithstanding the encouragement of denominational leaders, none of the members think the church could now do that. They would rather sell the building as a warehouse. Their concern about maintenance is reflected in an excerpt from the March minutes of the board: "Olivia Hess reports that the custodian has complained about finding taco sauce on the kitchen floor, a broken candle holder and dart marks on the cabinet doors in the Sunday-school office, and two M&Ms on the social hall floor. After discussion, it was decided that everyone would be more careful and try to pick up after themselves."

2. The total budget is realistically set at $16,000 for church operations. This barely covers utilities and maintenance, plus two luxuries: a part-time custodian ($1,900 per year) and a paid organist-choir director ($2,300 per year). Early hopes to exceed this amount because of the "free" interim had proved false. (See the budget and first-quarter performance in Table A-2.)

3. The church has deferred major maintenance: the organ and the heating plant could become major expenses. People worry out loud about these problems.

4. No older church members can leave a large bequest to St. John's; no one has that kind of wealth.

5. St. John's has a memorial fund amounting to $15,165. The fund has been built over the years by people's contributions to the fund in lieu of flowers when a member dies or on the occasion of an anniversary of a death. Olivia Hess has been successful in perpetuating the policy that none of the principal or interest can be spent on current expenses. None of the principal has been spent, and the only interest spent was for the burglar alarm.

6. Members are speaking encouragingly to former members about the church, and one family has returned. Others are thought to be ready to return, and might choose Easter Sunday as a date to come back. Attendance was up during the first three months of 1975.

7. St. John's also has a cash reserve in a savings account, which as of March 1975 amounted to $14,700, and it has a balance of $3,800 in a current checking account. This means its total cash assets amount to about $33,600, counting the memorial fund.

THE OPTIONS

1. Spend the church's savings and the memorial fund to hire a pastor for a three-year period. The pastor would be expected to redouble efforts to attract former members back to the church and to set up a program reminiscent of the church in its heyday. New efforts for attracting new members would be made. The existing members would agree to work hard with the pastor to form St. John's community support groups all over the metropolitan area where the members had moved. Also, there would be a full fellowship program for the church, including regular banquets and a weekly Sunday luncheon to serve members who lived some distance away. "Real" Sunday school would be revived.

This plan would turn things around for St. John's. "Of course it's risky," observes Jerry Williams, chair of the church board, "but it's the only chance for St. John's to become a vibrant, growing congregation." Obstacles to this plan are many, not the least of which is freeing the money in the memorial fund for this use. Privately, several people speculate that Olivia will take the board to court, if necessary, to

163

press her opposition to spending memorial-fund dollars. But Jerry and the other advocates of the plan propose to borrow the money from the fund and have prepared a repayment schedule with interest. "What better way to memorialize our forebears," he asks, "than to revitalize the church they loved?" If the plan fails, and the church closes, the sale of the church building and parsonage will more than repay the memorial-fund debt.

This plan has the support of the one family that has returned to St. John's, and several people who left because there was no Sunday school for their children say they like the plan. They will return if it is implemented.

2. Hire another interim pastor. The retired pastor who served St. Luke's Church up until it closed has indicated a willingness to become a part-time pastor of St. John's. He is a distinguished pastor with an impressive record of service. Most of the members know and like him. Moreover, he would not live in the parsonage, and it could be sold to raise necessary capital. Advocates of this plan say the parsonage could be sold for $16,000, according to a real-estate agent's estimate. Because this pastor knows the former members of the church, they will want to return. Also, he likes to make pastoral calls in homes, and that will be a definite plus. Older members especially support this plan because the pastor would provide the kind of ministry they want. While this plan might not be as successful in attracting former members, the proponents contend it is realistic and affordable.

3. A merger with two other congregations in the same part of the city has been informally considered for several years. The two churches, both of the same denomination, are respectively one mile and two miles away from St. John's. Both are stronger congregations and have larger buildings, and both have full-time pastors. St. John's is the most central of the three, however, and some members feel there is a chance that the united church would choose to keep their building and sell the other two.

Denominational leaders support this plan, and will provide an outside consultant to help the congregations work out a satisfactory plan of union. By combining the assets of the three churches there would be enough money to sponsor a home for the aged, a service for which there is demonstrated need in this part of the city. The members of all three churches are sympathetic to the idea even if a little overwhelmed by it.

Few members openly support this plan, principally because they think St. John's will be at a disadvantage in negotiations for a merged church. Mary Ellen Maxwell, the plan's main advocate, has persuaded the board to send three delegates to the Tri-Church Planning Commission, which is doing the preliminary feasibility study. The three churches, all weakened by the same demographic trends, could make one strong congregation with a multiple staff. If the plan is accepted, the pastors of the other two churches would provide services to St. John's until the time of actual church union.

4. The fourth course of action is openly advocated by no one. It was considered, however, albeit darkly. Members could simply find new churches on their own. The assets of the church could be given to the denomination for some appropriate ministry. In fact, this option has already been taken by people who have stopped coming to St. John's. Those who remain have high commitment to one another. "We must survive for the sake of our older members," Paul DeVeries asserts, and everyone agrees.

AN UPDATE ON ST. JOHN'S

The case as written describes St. John's situation in spring 1975. They hired the retired pastor and continued their discussion with the Tri-Church Planning Commission.

The urgency of their discussion increased when the heating plant broke down in the spring of 1976, and they faced a $20,000 replacement cost. The 96th anniversary of St. John's was its last; it merged with one of the two churches. The other of the two, refusing to give up its building, withdrew from the discussions. Months of planning went into bringing about the merger. The denomination provided expert consultation to aid the planning process. The merger was celebrated enthusiastically in both churches. St. John's memorial fund was to remain intact, but there were far too few assets for a home for the aged.

After only two years in the merged church, only one couple from St. John's still remains active, Paul and Evelyn De-Veries.

Some Questions for Analysis and Discussion

1. If in the months immediately before St. John's closed it had received a bequest of $35,000, what options would have been available to it? What would you advise? Would the options be greatly different if the bequest were $100,000?
2. Was there any way for St. John's to survive without such a bequest?
3. At what points in St. John's past, as far as can be told by the case material, could it have embarked on a different set of desired results with the effect of improving its long-term chances for survival?
4. What would you recommend be done with the church's assets at the time of its closing, based on its particular set of desired results? How would this differ if the recommendation were based on your perception of your church's set of desired results? That is, if your own church were to close, what should be done with the remaining assets? (The answer may give a clue to expressing your church's desired results.)
5. Using the idea of economic thresholds (see Chapter I, pages 26–27), describe the kind of thresholds through which St. John's has passed.

See also the general discussion questions on pages 28–29.

St. John's Church Sunday Worship Attendance Report, March 1974 and 1975

| | 1975 | | 1974 | |
	Members	Visitors	Members	Visitors
1st Sunday	84	0	74	0
2d Sunday	92	4	70	0
3d Sunday	89	4	85	0
4th Sunday	95	1	78	0
5th Sunday	105	7	85	0
TOTAL	465	16	392	0
Jan. & Feb. Total	681	23	580	6
1st Quarter Total	1146	39	972	6

TABLE A-2
St. John's Church Treasurer's Report, March 1975

RECEIPTS	March	To Date	Budget
General	$2,135.98	$3,931.35	$19,000.00
Contributions to denominational ministries	28.50	88.00	400.00
Missions by church organizations	—	—	—
Total budget receipts	$2,164.48	$4,019.35	$19,400.00
Other receipts	106.56	135.16	500.00
Total Receipts	$2,271.04	$4,154.61	$19,900.00
DISBURSEMENTS			
Salaries			
Pastor (interim)	$—	$—	$—
Pastor (Aug. through Dec.)	—	—	5,000.00
Minister of music	192.50	577.50	2,310.00
Organist Supply	—	—	50.00
Custodian	160.66	482.06	1,930.00
Pulpit supply (during pastor's illness)	—	125.00	100.00
Secretarial services	63.83	191.53	766.00

DISBURSEMENTS	March	To Date	Budget
Car allowance, pastor	56.76	56.76	250.00
Pension & relief	—	—	500.00
Health insurance	—	—	300.00
Utilities			
Gas	269.75	941.47	2,700.00
Electricity	70.94	219.92	850.00
Telephone	40.49	140.53	450.00
Water	—	8.60	50.00
Maintenance			
Insurance	—	—	1,600.00
Church	168.65	168.65	600.00
Parsonage	—	9.95	100.00
Operating expenses			
Postage	30.00	30.00	100.00
Music	—	26.32	50.00
Office	—	—	50.00
Church	—	112.65	500.00
Miscellaneous	47.27	64.66	100.00
Benevolences			
Denominational missions	—	—	400.00
Missions by church organizations	—	—	100.00
Hospital	—	—	100.00
Home for the aged	—	—	100.00
American Bible Society	—	—	50.00
Denominational support	—	—	100.00
Interdenominational work	—	—	50.00
Total disbursements			
(March 1975)	$1,100.85	$3,155.60	$19,256.00

OPERATING ACCOUNT

Balance on hand	
February 28, 1975	$2,630.05
Receipts for March 1975	2,271.04
Total	$4,901.09
Disbursements for March 1975	(1,100.85)
Balance on hand	
March 31, 1975	$3,800.24

SAVINGS ACCOUNT

Balance on hand	
February 28, 1975	$14,753.89
Receipts for March 1975	67.29
Total	$14,821.18
Disbursements for March 1975	—
Balance on hand	
March 31, 1975	$14,821.18

MEMORIAL FUND ACCOUNT

Balance on hand	
February 28, 1975	$14,691.93
Receipts for March 1975	400.00
Interest for March 1975	73.25
Balance on hand	
March 31, 1975	$15,165.18

FIRST CHURCH OF OLD TOWN*

An Overview of the Case

Like St. John's, First Church places high value on its past and tradition. There is, however, an important difference. Leaders in First Church are asking how to make the traditions live for new people. They are not trying to keep the traditions solely for the present members, and are hoping outsiders will help them do that. Furthermore, First Church also has a critically important resource that St. John's did not have—a modest endowment.

While it is too early to tell if the planning strategy taken by

---

*This case was prepared by Francis E. Ringer, professor, Lancaster Theological Seminary, as a basis for discussion rather than to illustrate effective or ineffective handling of a situation.

Pastor Stetson will have lasting effects, the preliminary signs are hopeful, with an increase in membership and attendance in 1981. In a sense, the church's decision to reject a merger with two other churches means its future is heavily dependent on such a planning venture and on the church's location.

The present leaders know the importance of attracting new members, but have as yet very little awareness of who these people might be or what effects their joining will have on the church's present goals. They want their tradition to serve as the basis for reaching out in new directions, but are not yet sure how to do this. The leaders who participate in the dialogue that follows may encounter some resistance among other members who have high personal desire for things at First Church to remain as they presently are.

Using the decision points of Diagram 2, p. 79, the situation of First Church may be described as follows.

A. They might increase income by recruiting new members, but present members are probably giving at near maximal levels.
B. It has developed an endowment program that is presently producing an acceptable rate of income. The leaders are aware of additional bequests that will come their way in the future.
C. The leaders are moving quickly to improve their budget-making process, to make up for previous poor management. They are caring for maintenance deferred in the past, including cleaning and repointing the bricks.
D. Clearly, the main desired results of this church are under pressure to change. Raising questions about how a church's traditions serve new people and new occasions will probably lead to new and unfamiliar expressions of the tradition.
E. As with the case of St. John's, this church's location is of critical importance for determining its future constituency. By rejecting an invitation to merge with two other churches and to move to a suburb where growth would be virtually assured, First Church cast its lot with the "downtown" constituency without fully knowing what the implications might be. Fortunately, the downtown is experiencing a kind of renaissance, and new residents have a popular appreciation for history.

171

F. The church has leaders capable of analyzing the options and of making informed decisions.

Key Leaders

"This meeting may be far more important than we imagined when we scheduled it routinely several months ago. I suspect that we of First Church have come to a point of major change in direction, something of a turnaround. What we recommend to the Consistory in October may well start First Church upon a new epoch in its long history here."

With this pensive comment, Henry Stetson, pastor of First Church, began the deliberations of the advisory committee of four. Theirs was the responsibility of formulating recommendations for both program and budget priorities for the coming year. They were to attempt to summarize and focus the deliberations of many church members in "cabinet" workshops, present priority possibilities to the Consistory, and exercise various degrees of leadership personally in carrying out the decisions finally enacted by the congregation in January in response to the program and budget presented by the Consistory. Although it would be January before the adoption of the budget, the program priorities recommended by this committee and refined by the Consistory would provide guidance to the life of the organization of First Church from October on.

The four persons who met in the pastor's study in historic First Church brought with them a variety of interests in the life the church. Henry Stetson had been pastor of the congregation only one year at the time of this September 1978 meeting. He had clearly understood his starting point to be that of seeking to revive interest and activity in First Church members, a large number of whom had drifted into apathy and indifference in recent years. Along with this task, Henry knew he had to increase the outreach of the congregation through evangelism and service. In his own priorities, this search for "new blood" arose from a commitment to the central commission of the church of Jesus Christ. For him the first reason for evangelism was to present Jesus Christ to unchurched persons, encouraging and challenging them to focus their lives upon the kingdom life. He thought of those in the kingdom as caught up in the vision and mission of Christians seeking to be faithful to the person of Christ, both within the church and within the community. Henry knew that a salutary by-product of evangelism by Christians was membership growth, which First Church needed.

John Clarkson was a lifelong member of First Church. Now in his early 50s, he had grown up with the traditions of the church, traditions firmly supported and treasured by his parents before him. He had become an officer in his father's business shortly after college, and upon his father's retirement had become head of the company, which remained essentially a family business although it employed about thirty persons. The company provided cleaning services to businesses and private homes. Conservative by disposition, John had become intrigued by new possibilities and a new vision of the church to which Henry had introduced him. He now appreciated denominational ties, even though he continued to have reservations about some aspects of denominational activity. He was growing daily to appreciate that the church is far more than First Church. The larger vision led him to see his own traditions as both enriching and limiting. He wanted to share the richness of both his faith and his tradition, but in the business world he had long since learned that traditions are meaningless to those outside their influence. First Church, he was coming to see, would need to relate to present interests and needs of people outside its membership, would need to mount programs and especially an evangelistic outreach directed to interests of people not within the present traditions. Perhaps those won to a Christian life would come to appreciate the traditions of First Church; perhaps new styles or variations within the old styles would have to be

173

given places within the hallowed traditions if new persons were to find a home in the congregation. As one who worked with church funds, John knew that "new blood" was necessary to meet the expanding budget.

James Rockingham was a secondary-school principal and young in manners and thinking for his 50 years. He presently chaired the Stewardship Committee. Jim had come to First Church when he married. Although he had grown to appreciate many traditions over the years, he believed traditions were helpful to people but should be neither inhibiting nor limiting. As he put it once, "Today's traditions were yesterday's attempts to meet what were contemporary needs. They were not answers to all future problems forever." At the same time he was convinced that present members needed to be loyal "or get off the boat," that the church needed to apply traditional standards to keep the membership limited to those active and financially supportive of First Church, or else the rolls would be filled with inactives and all members would be deceived about the actual vitality of the congregation.

Beatrice Edwards had for many years served as the secretary to the pastors of First Church. Within the year she had relinquished that post to become lay assistant for visitation. Acquainted with the membership of First Church from her years of association with them, she was extremely valuable to Henry as he became familiar with his new tasks. She was sensitive to many of the feelings of the members about affairs in recent years within the life of the congregation. Her wisdom helped Henry avoid unintentionally alienating persons as he went about developing his own style of ministry. A longtime supporter of First Church traditions, she cautioned against sudden and disruptive changes that could dismay some members. Honored by the members for years, Beatrice was valued increasingly by the pastor as he worked with her advice and counsel.

These four brought together a wealth of experience and of insights into the past and present of First Church. Upon them fell now the heavy responsibility of framing priority proposals for the future of this historic church.

History of First Church

First Church had been born from a gathering of early German settlers of the Reformed tradition in 1729. They founded a congregation officially in 1734, soon erecting a log church of modest dimensions. In 1758 they erected a stone church, replaced in 1850 by the present brick building of impressive design and size, capable of seating nearly a thousand people. On the same site since 1734, First Church had amicably funded the beginnings of two other congregations over its long life when different interests threatened a division of the congregation. One new congregation was born of a difference in church-school philosophy, and one of a difference over the language to be used in worship, German or English. This ironic spirit, part of the First Church tradition for nearly 250 years, was tested again in the late 1960s and the early 1970s when the new congregations entered into merger negotiations and invited First Church to share the process. All three churches would leave their present buildings and erect a new edifice west of the city. After much deliberation, the congregation voted overwhelmingly, with 75 percent of the members voting, to stay in the center of the city and seek to continue its ministry to its present members and also to endeavor to win new persons from the changing populace.

The city of Oldtown was one of the nation's oldest and from colonial days until the 1950s had maintained the same city limits. Much of the open space filled gradually with buildings; old buildings were sometimes replaced or remodeled. In the 1950s the city began a major program of renovation, at first removing historic buildings but soon changing its approach to that of restoration. The city around First Church began to look alive and thriving, particularly attracting two classes of people into residence nearby. Old properties, some from the colonial era, were restored and refurbished as attractive town-houses. Many single men and women and young couples were purchasing them as a base for an urbane life-style. The other class of people were the retired, who lived in old homes converted to apartments or in new high-rise apartments. All presented problems of access for evangelistic visitation.

Concurrent with the period of inner-city reconstruction was the long pastorate of Henry Stetson's predecessor from 1955 to 1977. It was during these years that several significant events occurred. With renovation in process all around, the pastor urged the purchase of a new parsonage in a wealthy residential section to the west of the city in order that he and his family need no longer live next to the church. This was interpreted by some as an attempt to climb socially above the membership. For years the issue of the parsonage simmered; it flared again near the end of his pastorate, when he involved the congregation in a controversy over the proposed sale of the historic parsonage at the church site. The final decision to keep the building was in large part settled by the intervention of the Historical Commission of the city.

During the controversy over the historic parsonage edifice, another issue fomented much discussion. In the early years of the century a family had left to the congregation a sturdy Victorian townhouse of great size. A trust fund was also established to maintain the structure and provide for church members of limited means a place to live and regular meals after they had retired. This home had come to be a significant factor in the life and ministry of First Church. State regulations began to create problems for the traditional operation of the home. Again the congregation was cast into turmoil. The pastor, as director of the trust fund, proposed the relocation of the guests and the sale of the home, with the proceeds to be added to the trust. Indigent aged would be aided by the fund to enter church homes elsewhere. Some members urged the search for creative alternatives to permit keeping the home even if it required building wings or adjacent buildings and converting the present edifice to apartments not covered by nursing-home regulations. Ultimately, the home was sold and the guests relocated; many members felt that this was accomplished with little regard for the will of the membership. No longer were the residents of the home part of the life of the congregation, and many members of advancing years felt betrayed by the loss of the home that would have kept them close to community and church. Shortly after the controversies over the old parsonage and the retirement home, the pastor retired and petitioned that he be granted a pension as part of the church budget. For some this was the last indignity, and they exited the church to join the ranks of those who had already withdrawn over the issues of parsonage and retirement home. Among those who remained was a mood of apathy fed by the experience of powerlessness as they saw cherished aspects of the life and ministry of First Church dismantled or threatened by those they had trusted to defend and preserve them.

The Challenges Awaiting Pastor Stetson

When Henry Stetson arrived in September 1977, he entered with full awareness of a very troubled and endangered congregation. Although many listings of problems were possible, five key issues epitomized the plight of First Church. First, there were many disheartened members and a pervading negativism. Second, some were clinging almost desperately to traditions, especially in liturgy, apparently in hope of bringing back times past. Third, First Church had largely lost its visibility in the community as either historic site or living community with a mission. Fourth, the congregation and leaders were frustrated by powerlessness before the closed doors of townhouses, apartments, and high rises when they endeavored to mount programs of evangelism. Fifth, there was a frightening realization that former financial patterns had now failed and that the life, ministry, and hallowed traditions

177

were in jeopardy, with many ardent supporters of tradition seeing their ability to maintain the familiar slipping beyond their financial capacities.

In some respects this fifth factor had been integral to the other four as well. Over many years the financial program of First Church and the traditions of First Church were largely separate phenomena. The bulk of the membership provided very modest amounts of financial support. A few large contributors provided the guarantee of each year's budget. Proceeds from endowments were a further aid to the financial program. The liturgical and social life of the congregation stood as virtually unchangeable, and members participated in these as their rights and prerogatives regardless of their financial responsibility toward First Church. Now inflation in the 1970s had elevated the budget, while death had removed some large contributors. Additional financial support had been lost with the withdrawal from active participation of those alienated by parsonage and retirement-home issues. Henry Stetson faced a membership composed of many who viewed the church as a resource for their comfort at their discretion and of the relatively few who saw the financial aspects of the church as in any significant way their responsibility. By 1978 the church had lost 19 percent of the 1965 membership, and yet in 1978 it had spent 55 percent more than in 1965. This dollar increase had barely allowed First Church to keep pace with its present program and had not signaled growth or advance in ministry. Moreover, the increase in support had been provided by several members who by 1978 had either died or were reduced to living with the economic restraints of pension incomes. Budget problems were threatening to become more acute at a time when new programs were much needed for outreach leading to growth.

Pastor Stetson's Strategy

Henry Stetson began his ministry at First Church by affirming the congregation as he found it. Shortly after his arrival he engaged with the Consistory in a study of the life and goals of the church. From this evolved gatherings of leaders and interested members in loosely organized "cabinet workshops." These workshops began with Bible study, asking seriously how to keep close or move closer to the biblical style for congregational life and mission. The cabinet drew up suggested goals for a year, and the Consistory and congregation in annual meeting ratified and sought to implement them. As a valuable element in this process, the Consistory and pastor reviewed the membership, classifying each person according to categories of involvement in the life of the congregation. The cabinet set some goals in relation to certain categories within the membership. By the second year the Consistory, cabinet, and congregation would be able to mark significant gains in their pursuit of specific goals. The active church members had grown to be more precise in their thinking about church members of differing degrees of commitment. This led to increased realism in formulating goals for the coming year.

By lifting up among the people the implications of the Bible, the implications of First Church traditions, the spiritual and practical needs of the members, and the needs of the adjacent community, Henry Stetson had quietly broadened the understanding of an increasing number of members. To live only for themselves no longer was the principal intention of a growing corps of persons. The entire process had begun building ownership and responsibility into the thinking of active First Church members. An atmosphere of openness and trust slowly displaced the negativism and apathy. There was still a long way to go, but Henry and others were encouraged to think that something of a turnaround had already been achieved.

Which Way to Tomorrow?

"I suspect," said Jim Rockingham in response to Henry Stetson's opening comment, "that we are asked to suggest to the Consistory possible ways to go into tomorrow. Wouldn't it be nice to have a yellow brick road waiting?"

"Perhaps that's been our problem," suggested John Clarkson. "Ever since I can remember we've assumed that someone or something would come along and help us out of tight places at a minimum demand upon the majority of us. But I don't think we can count on that now."

Beatrice Edwards objected to this. "Be careful, John, that you don't confuse faith in God with sitting back and 'letting George do it.' There's been a strong faith among us here for the many years I've known First Church. In that faith we have been strong in our confidence in prayer and in our trust in God, who hears our prayers. That has been and continues to be the backbone of our liturgy, this faith we have inherited from our parents and their parents, this faith we express in the same liturgy they used. I firmly believe also that our liturgy is the best training in prayer our children can get. I am not ashamed to trust in God and to accept the solutions God sends us."

John defended himself: "That's not quite what I meant. I share your belief in trusting God to be with us in solving problems, but what I was trying to say was that we must not sit back and neglect doing what we can with the human skills God has given us. We must help ourselves all we can, and I see in that an expression of faith, because we believe God will use and augment what we do."

"I agree, John," said Jim. "Beatrice, I think your views of the liturgy are valid for many here, but I don't think you realize that some are left out of the richness you find in our traditions. As one who came into the church by marriage, as it were, I never really grew up in this liturgy. My faith in God and prayer had formed elsewhere in a different way. For me the liturgy at times is rich, and at times leaves me cold. I know that distresses you, but it's true."

"Yes," said John, "I have gradually come to agree with Jim, Beatrice. I can see how our liturgy may even be a stumbling block for new people, especially if we offer little or no varia-

180

tion to appeal to them where they are, where they come from."

"Liturgy is not designed to appeal to humans, but to be appropriate for God!" exclaimed Beatrice.

"I'm sorry to interrupt," said Henry. "You're all correct in what you say, and probably each is guilty of overstating or omitting elements that belong to the matter you've been discussing. However, we must get on to our assignment. As we turn to the issue of priorities, please keep in mind what has just been said among you. This may give us strong hints about the decisions we need to make."

"Pastor, what do you see as key issues?" asked Jim. "In order to get started, how about suggesting some ideas for us?"

"Well, all right. We must begin somewhere with someone. I guess it might as well be me. Let me suggest some factors with which I believe we must deal seriously as we face the future. I think I can list them from some notes I jotted down." He proceeded to read them his "laundry list."

1. Financial priorities: How do we allocate them to preserve buildings *and* develop members as stronger Christians *and* reach out to new people?
    a. What do we need to do to help members grow in commitment, involvement, and mission for Christ? What money do we need, and how shall we spend it? Retreats? Specialists? Program funds for experimental activities?
    b. How do we reach out to new people, and why? Do we want "fellow members" or only contributors? Will we invest in special events for new prospects? Will we put our members, at our expense, in places where they can "infiltrate" for us?
2. Human priorities: How do we continue to develop our sense of identity as members of First Church?
    a. How can we understand our fellow members without falling victim to pride or vindictiveness?
    b. What can we do to involve more people in our goals, sharing a widening sense of ownership?

181

c. What can we do to preserve tradition and speak with newness to our own day? What can we do to preserve the rich liturgy of the past and lift new people in worship experiences that express who *they* are?
　3. What is our *first* priority?
　　a. Rejection of merger: To preserve historic buildings? To minister to people around us?
　　b. Concentration on tradition: To carry us into the future? To help us reconstruct a past?
　　c. Reorientation of life: Are we to help people find the joy of new life in Christ, pouring our financial and human resources into both evangelism and the nurturing of members, old and new?

"Those are my starting points," said Henry, "and I think I'm prepared to suggest we reduce our expenditures on building restoration and increase our investment in people. I'm willing to experiment with evangelism and with at least some variations in liturgy to make newcomers feel at home."

"I can feel some real challenge there to the way I've been thinking," said John. "I also see possibilities for exciting new experiences as a member of First Church. How can we keep the best of the past and appeal to our own day?"

"Let's be careful we don't sell out to newness," pleaded Beatrice. "The liturgy is our heart."

"I think we have that exciting new experience beginning already," said Jim. "The fact that we're not simply trying to do just what we've always done before may be a hopeful sign of newness. Let's get going! I'll suggest a priority to get the process going. Let's cut building-related items to a minimum, reduce the music budget, and mount a program of outreach to the high rises and the single people in the townhouses."

Some Questions for Analysis and Discussion

1. What immediate decisions would you recommend to First Church? What priorities or desired new results would you suggest?

2. What recommendations would you make to First Church when its endowment reaches $500,000? $1,000,000?
3. To what extent, if any, has inflation hurt this church?
4. How might recession hurt or help this church, for example, reduction in housing starts?

See also the general questions for discussion on pages 28–29.

NEVER SAY DIE*

An Overview of the Case

This case presents the story of a new church founded by a sponsoring congregation with the possibility that over a period of years members of the older congregation would shift their membership to the new church. At least the new church, Reston Baptist, would provide some continuation of the older church should hard times befall First Church.

Reston Baptist Church is an example of a congregation that initially failed to develop a clear understanding of what results it really wanted. It accepted, largely uncritically, the expectations that the parent congregation had for it. Its expressed desired results were not its own. This parent-child relation-

*This case was prepared by Marjorie Hall Davis, adjunct faculty, Hartford Seminary, as a basis for discussion rather than to illustrate effective or ineffective handling of a situation.

ship between the two churches even prevented the Reston church from knowing what its financial situation was or from taking responsibility for it. Its situation would be analogous to an unfortunate child whose parents announce unexpectedly that they cannot afford to keep the child any longer.

Reston Baptist can, of course, survive in some form for a long time. Some very difficult financial decisions will have to be made, however. Moreover, Reston will need to develop its own expectations about itself.

Using the outline of decision points, Diagram 2, page 79, the case of Reston Baptist Church may be summarized as follows:

A. Present members might be motivated to give more money. They have not been challenged with any clear reasons for their contributions.
B. There is little opportunity for income from other sources, especially given the poor financial circumstances of the parent church.
C. Members are unsure what resources they need to purchase because they are unsure what results they desire.
D. The rethinking of their main goals is underway with the consideration of three alternative strategies for the future.
E. The constituency for the church, a potentially booming suburb plus members from the parent church, failed to develop as anticipated.
F. There are some signs that leadership is more likely to give in to frustration rather than to make necessary decisions.

Parent and Child Congregations

Gary Fuller's concluding words echoed in Steve Howard's ears as he glanced around the room at those who had gathered to make a decision about the survival of the Baptist church in Reston. As its pastor, Steve had worked closely with the small congregation for two years, trying to help its members understand the implications of their dwindling number and failure to become financially self-sufficient. He had arranged for Gary to meet with the church's steering committee to describe his impressive but unsuccessful attempt to start a Protestant church of another denomination in Reston. Steve shared the committee's amazement at the scope of Gary's media campaign. Steve had expected, however, that Gary's lack of success, in spite of his thorough and thoughtful efforts and his record of two previous successful new church starts, would help the committee to understand the improbability of success of a "last-ditch" effort on its part. Then, as Gary shared the massive scope of his media campaign, Steve had sensed the growing excitement in the room. And Steve was completely taken by surprise when Gary concluded his remarks by enthusiastically urging the group, "I couldn't do it, but you've got what it takes. Go to it!"

Steven Howard had accepted the call to Reston in 1977, moving into the parsonage with his wife and two young daughters, aged five and eight. Steve had felt affirmed in his two previous positions, which covered some 10 years; he accepted the new position, however, because he was "intrigued with the history of the Reston church" and with the "different kind of challenge" it offered. The history of the Reston church was linked to that of First Baptist Church in Wallaceboro, the church that had been and continued to be its "parent," having established the Reston church in 1965. He admitted to himself that he had walked in "with his eyes wide open," having been told of the frustration of his two immediate predecessors and being aware of his call to "show progress in two years."

FIRST BAPTIST CHURCH

Founded in 1875, the parent church was described in the report of a study by the national mission office in 1962 as having a "long and glorious history" in the industrial city of Wallaceboro, Massachusetts. Prior to the time of the study, however, First Church had steadily and dramatically lost membership, which had decreased from 928 to 391 between 1947 and 1960. In addition, it faced serious leadership difficulties; almost half its church leaders were over 60 years of age, with relatively few young people and few families. A middle-class Protestant church in the midst of a now "over-churched" city of 140,000, it had been functioning as if it were a traditional church in a stable community, competing with other Protestant churches for the small remaining Protestant population as white middle-class Protestants retreated to the suburbs. Meanwhile, its community had become unstable and nonmiddle-class. The national mission report predicted, "If it continues its present course, this church in ten or fifteen years may be in deep trouble, almost to the point of death. Without a ministry more oriented toward the social needs of its immediate community, First Church does not have an optimistic future." The church was commended for its social awareness because it had given 28 percent of its total income to missions. It was also noted that the church received about 30 percent of its income from endowment funds. The report strongly recommended that First Church consider merger with Center Baptist Church, another American Baptist congregation in Wallaceboro. Relocation of the church was also mentioned.

A merger was explored. Steve recalled hearing the oft-repeated explanation that Center Church had a lot of people but very little money, First Church had a lot of money but few people, and each group was afraid of the other's power. In a preliminary vote one church voted for the merger and the other against. Six months later both churches reversed their votes and the idea of merger was dropped.

THE BAPTIST CHURCH IN RESTON

When a 1962 study of a joint committee of the Massachusetts Council of Churches projected that there was room for one more Protestant church in Reston, First Church was asked by the Baptist State Convention to sponsor a mission church there.

Reston was at that time a growing suburb of Wallaceboro with a highly mobile population of 8,500. Roman Catholic, United Church of Christ, and Episcopal churches were well established there, as well as two Jewish congregations.

Although some thought was given to moving the entire church to Reston, decisions were made to sell First Church's large and aging downtown church structure, to build a smaller, more efficient structure near its original location, and to start a mission church in Reston, seven miles away. Sale of the old building would provide $125,000 for the new church in Wallaceboro, and First Church would borrow $100,000 from the national mission board for the structure in Reston.

John Andrews, the pastor of First Church in Wallaceboro, had shared with Steve his understanding of his congregation's action. "It was their intent to keep all the options open. They were trying to feel their way along, not to leave anybody out, and to see what would happen." Staying in Wallaceboro avoided excluding those older people who did not drive and could not get to Reston, as well as a Chinese congregation that had met in the church with its own pastor on Sunday afternoons for the past 75 years or so. There was also the thought that the situation might eventually reverse, with the congregation of the suburbs becoming the main church and the downtown church becoming the mission.

Steve knew the history of the Reston church by heart, as he had spent many hours in the past two years reflecting on the events that led up to the present.

1964: First Baptist Church purchased a site in Reston with a parsonage and 3.6 acres at a cost of $5,000, and the pastor of First Church moved into the parsonage.

1965: In February, First Church voted to establish a new church in Reston with its pastor serving both congregations. On Easter Sunday the first service was held in the parsonage.

1965–67:	The pastor held Sunday services in the parsonage, with 45 to 50 people who filled the living room, the dining room, and the stairwell. He also held a service in the Wallaceboro church later each Sunday morning.
1967:	The Reston building was completed and dedicated in April.
1967–77:	There were two changes of pastors, with each serving the Wallaceboro and Reston congregations. The Chinese congregation continued with its own pastor, with primary funding from First Church.
1977:	Steve Howard was called as pastor of the Reston church.
1979:	The final mortgage payment was made.

For a while all reports agreed that the mission church in the suburbs was going well. John Andrews told Steve, "Parishioners in the downtown church saw Reston as providing leadership for us on the boards of finance, deacons, and Christian education, some financial support, and our potential for the future." One feature of the First Church-Reston relationship was an integrated board and budget structure. By 1977, membership on the major boards consisted of half from the Wallaceboro congregation, and one-fourth each from the Reston and Chinese congregations. In addition to paying off the Reston mortgage, First Church continued to pay the operating deficit for the Reston church, but not directly. There was an arrangement whereby First Church sent money to the home mission board, designated for Reston, and it came back into the joint budget for the two congregations. In 1978 and 1979 these funds amounted to $11,400 annually.

There had been ups and downs in the Reston congregation. At no time did it have more than 75 members, and the general trend had been one of decline since the founding pastor left in 1970. In 1976, Peter Zito, who worked with the Reston congregation during his last two years of seminary, wrote in his report: "In terms of survival and long-term health, both First Church and Reston congregations are at a crisis point. . . . What pastor in his right mind would step into the situation as it now exists? It is heavily stacked against progress in any direction." He suggested a plan for progressive autonomy of the Reston congregation, including a pastor of its own, a "church-development type of pastoral leadership—a sharp, sensitive person who will involve himself in Reston alone and do a lot of door knocking. It will be tough going, but the struggle may breathe new life and strength into this congregation."

And that, Steve recalled, is where he came in. When its pastor resigned, First Church authorized additional withdrawals from endowment principal for two years to provide a separate pastor for the Reston congregation "to see if it would fly." Steve came to Reston in September 1977, and John Andrews, a man in his 60s with considerable experience, came to Wallaceboro in November of the same year.

By 1977 the town of Reston had grown to 15,000. The building inspector reported about 30 new house starts per year, and town records revealed that one out of three residents had changed houses in the past five years. Average family income was $18,682 in the 1970 census, with 25 percent of the population professional people, 16 percent clerical, and 16 percent management and administrative.

Steve soon learned that most of his congregation did not know how much it was costing to run the church or just where the money was coming from. Steve also learned that the budget was buried within the First Church's budget, overseen by a joint board of finance and a single treasurer. Steve also found out that 92 percent of the mission giving was designated for Reston. Thus, he reflected, "we in Reston have no way of giving to mission; we *are* the mission."

During Steve's first year at Reston, average attendance increased from 18 to 24, and there was a net gain of three members and three active nonmembers, making a total of 30. As a result of 475 visits to new residents in the community, nine individuals or families came to church one or more times, and one became involved in the life of the church. The

Reston congregation was happy to have Steve do the calling, but he could not find anyone to go on a follow-up visit. He heard one person say, "We don't like to go calling."

He had preached on church growth and had tried to help the congregation develop a vision for itself and begin to take responsibility for making some concrete steps toward growth, spiritual as well as numerical. He had shared with the members his belief that "a church will grow if it provides its members with opportunities for personal spiritual growth and opportunities for ministry, that is, witnessing to their faith and righting the wrongs around us. We need to pray together to discover what God wants us to do. I have a vision of making the Reston church a demonstration of what God can do through people who are really willing to trust him." Pledging increased by 71 percent to a total of $5,000. In his report to the church at its annual meeting in March 1979 he had warned, "We must not forget that our position is *very* precarious."

John Andrews had been open in his praise of Steve. To a parishioner he had remarked, "That the anticipated growth did not come about is not because we chose poorly in the pastor we selected. Steve is doing everything he can. It's simply the dynamics of the situation. They are closing schools in Reston now. Take out the Catholic and Jewish population (80–90 percent), take strong United Church of Christ and Episcopal churches, and I don't see much in the next 10 years that is going to change the picture."

HAROLD STODDARDS' MEMOS

In August 1978, Steve received his first memo from Harold Stoddards. Harold, described by his friends as "sharp as a tack at 93," was a former president of the Harrisboro Railroad and a member of First Church's Endowment Funds Committee, a "triumvirate of businessmen and bankers." This three-member committee, as authorized by the church bylaws, had complete control of the invested funds of the church, and the portion of the bylaws relating to its authority could not be changed without its consent. Furthermore, if a member died or resigned, a replacement was selected by the two other members.

In the memo, Harold pointed out how critical the state of First Church's finances was becoming, especially with the loss of income incurred from using the principal of the endowment fund at the rate of $48,000 per year. He also called attention to the market value of the endowment fund, which was $411,236 as of June 1978.

During a visit with Harold, Steve was told that the Reston church could not technically receive any funding from First Church if it were to become independent, because "the major endowment fund was restricted to use by First Baptist Church of Wallaceboro." Harold urged Steve to seek State Convention funds to subsidize Reston while maintaining the interdependent role of the church boards. Believing that a sense of paternalism fostered by this arrangement of dependency was both unhealthy and inevitable under the present structure, Steve attempted to find a way for Reston to become an independent unit and still receive First Church's financial support. His efforts proved fruitless.

In May 1979, Steve received Harold Stoddards' second memo, marked "Confidential." It read: "Before January 1, 1981, the endowment fund must stop financing the deficit in the Reston extension. . . . I have concluded that we have done more than our share to plan a witness for the American Baptist denomination in Reston, and after January 1, 1981, the fund will not pay any further Reston extension deficits."

Steve knew the situation all too well. The total budget of the First, Reston, and Chinese congregations was $116,000 for 1980. The pledges and loose offerings from the three congregations were about $21,000 (with $5,500 from Reston), so the downtown church was having to find almost $100,000 a year, taking $48,000 from endowment-fund principal as well as all its endowment income (now down to $31,000 per year). First Church in Wallaceboro, with a resident membership of

90 and pledges of $14,500 from 39 individuals or families, was subsidizing the Chinese congregation (with 30 active members and pledges of $1,000) as well as its own operating deficit. Even without subsidizing Reston, it would still need to take $25,600 a year from investment principal. It was obvious that without some change, in less than 10 years there would be no money and no church—neither downtown, nor Chinese, nor Reston.

Although Harold Stoddards had expressed his belief that the State Convention should now take over the support of the Reston church, the Convention's response to the request was that it was already supporting three floundering churches and could not support a fourth. John had asked, "If it's going to be a deficit-financing operation after 15 years, who could afford the deficit? Should anybody?"

Steve obtained Harold's permission to make the financial information public. Along with the presentation of the data, Steve read a statement to the Reston congregation in September 1979: "The status quo cannot continue. I see three alternatives: (1) increase our giving by 500 percent, (2) fold up and fade away, or (3) find other sources of funding." Steve remembered the shock and confusion that followed his presentation: "We didn't know!" "Why didn't someone tell us before now?" "If we had known, we would have started working on our growth campaign earlier."

THE STEERING COMMITTEE

The State Convention had agreed to share the cost of a consultant to help assess the Reston situation. A steering committee of five members from the Reston church, plus Steve, was formed to work with Dr. George Allenson, a professional church consultant, skilled in the analysis of congregational growth and decline. From the first meeting, Steve was aware that George had been received by the Reston congregation with differing expectations. He and George were in agreement that George's role was, as stated in his contract, to help the Reston congregation structure a process that reaches a decision regarding the viability of an American Baptist ministry and presence in Reston that is faithful to the Gospel and to the realities and contingencies of the Reston situation, and is sensitive to the lives and commitment of Reston membership . . . the end product to be a recommendation to the First Baptist Church of Wallaceboro.

In a letter to the executive minister in December, Steve reported:

The survey of the work is well underway with a six-member steering committee deeply involved at the emotional level now. Every time we bring in a person who has not been to a meeting it takes an hour or two for that person to begin to grasp the situation. All six of us have now had this baptism, but it will be necessary for the rest of the congregation to undergo it as time goes on. Two of the five haven't said much, and they're the two who are on the Board of Finance and have been around for years. The three people who are newest to the church are displaying a "never say die" fighting spirit and an eagerness and determination which would gladden the heart of any pastor, at least in normal circumstances. I still don't have a clear sense of what is the best option. I'm trying to get in mind what all the possible options are.

By December, the steering committee had not acted on George Allenson's recommendation to gather data on the community as a step to exploring alternative ministries. George shared with Steve his feeling that the members of the steering committee "don't want to talk about anything but church growth and independence from First Church." In response, Steve suggested the committee might be helped by learning what Gary Fuller had done.

Steve had known Gary for the 13 months Gary had been trying to start a Congregational church in Reston. He had not viewed Gary's church as competing with his, and the two men had shared ideas as well as frustrations. Although he came with considerable experience, Gary was not able to gather a congregation and had requested that his denomination pull him out. As Steve and George planned the January 16 meeting of the steering committee, George had remarked, "The probability is certainly low for numerical growth and financial viability. If Gary Fuller can't help the congregation understand this, no one will!"

THE JANUARY 16 MEETING

Present besides Steve, George, and Gary were the five members of the steering committee. After an opening prayer, Steve reminded the committee that the purpose of the meeting was to evaluate the ideas that had come from an earlier meeting of the congregation and to decide on one specific option for the congregation to consider. He also reminded them that part of George's stated role was "to keep us realistic."

George began by presenting the first of three scenarios, "Rapid Growth Campaign," explaining what would be required. (See "A Series of Critical Events," pp. 196–99.) Sam Martin was excited about it, saying, "There's no place to go but up. I like a challenge." Anne Holmes added, "I'm optimistic. I want this thing to work." George estimated its probability of long-term success to be less than 5 percent. Tom Hendrix, Helen Lawrence, and Frank Kirby were silent.

Next George presented a plan to "Reorganize Under Special Ministry to the Community," outlining a possible budget and sources of funding. Steve sensed Anne's growing impatience and saw that this was shared by others. There were no comments or questions. When George started to present the third scenario, a plan to "Disband with Dignity and Purpose," (see p. 201), Sam interrupted him. "That's negative thinking," he charged. "You were hired to help us grow!" Anne added, "We can always disband if it doesn't work." They did not let George finish.

Gary was then asked to make his presentation. Almost item for item his plan paralleled George's proposal for a rapid-growth campaign. There was one difference. Gary had attempted to gather his congregation in a school. "Without a building, new people don't feel a sense of permanence," he said. "You have a building, I think you could do it!"

Amid the enthusiastic chorus of responses from the parishioners, Steve struggled with his own response to Gary's suggestion.

A Series of Critical Events

On May 29, Steve Howard returned home after a meeting of the steering committee. He sat at his desk and picked up his journal. As he slowly turned the pages, he recalled the events of the past five months.

January 16. The committee voted tonight to recommend a rapid growth campaign to the Reston congregation. I was so sure that they would be ready to look at other options after hearing Gary. I know George was as dumbfounded as I was, but as he walked out the door, George said, "Hey, we just might do it!"

January 20. Even in the face of a lot of hard work ahead, the general attitude seems to be "We *must* give it one more deliberate and vigorous try." When I presented my proposal (combining George's suggestions with other resources) to the steering committee, Sam said it was the best thing he'd seen yet. Some (not all) said, "We're ready." The committee agreed to call me by Thursday with any suggestions for change. Then we'd present it to everyone next Sunday morning.

January 28. We sent a letter today to the Reston congregation, asking everyone to sign up for one or two task forces. We need people for a calling task force and a worship church school/building task force.

February 12. George met with the steering committee to-

196

night. We set some goals for growth. George pushed us hard to set some deadlines. March will be too soon, but we agreed to report to First Church in June.

March 9. Anne gave a report at the annual meeting of First Church in Wallaceboro, asking for an extension until June 9, when a final recommendation from the Reston church would be made. The reason for the request was that the Reston members felt they were on the verge of a growth spurt and needed time to test this further. Of course, extra time was granted. The downtown people really don't want to see Reston die, and they don't want to be unsupportive of the efforts of the Reston congregation. They really saw us as their "ace in the hole."

But I know that John is concerned. He wants to be sure that a firm decision will be made by June 9 and has said that if the Reston church can't make it, then the whole church will have to decide. He told me that he had a gut feeling that the Reston people are not ready, and will never be ready, to say, "Let's close the church." John and I both know that First Church in Wallaceboro must still face some hard decisions about its own future. There aren't more than 30 active members left, and most of them are over 60 years old.

April 28. George warned me that the Reston people might not have enough energy to follow through, and that seems to be the case. Everyone signed up for the task forces, but they just don't seem to have the time for meetings. Some have worked on the building, but the calling committee hasn't had a meeting yet.

I'm discouraged, yet there seems to be a good spirit in the congregation toward me, and it felt good to hear Tom say that as long as we are together, it was important to him that I was bringing the Word of God to them. It also helps to know that George, in a letter to John, affirmed me and said that I have carried on a "most admirable ministry." He said that my gifts of energy, expertise, patience, and faithfulness need to be affirmed and appreciated.

May 6. Tonight Frank, who is on both the steering committee and the board of finance, recommended closing the church by June 30. Sam still wants to keep it going; he doesn't like negative thinking. Anne wants to continue until the end of 1980. Helen said little, but she knew that others had seen her crying at last week's meeting of the board of finance. Tom was struggling with it, perhaps ready to look at the facts. I talked a little about faithful use of resources and how we'd be leaven in other churches, and proposed a plan for a closedown. I gave my assessment of the energies of the congregation as very low and gave some figures for keeping the church building going. I knew Sam didn't like what I was saying. At his suggestion, the committee is going to meet without me. I think that's a wise decision.

May 22. The steering committee has met twice without me. I learned that Anne is writing a report to read to the Reston congregation on Sunday, and she has accepted my offer to work with her on it. She invited my family over Saturday evening.

May 25. Anne read the statement at the end of the service, a critically important step. The committee has concluded that we cannot continue—that we must recommend closing in our report to the whole church downtown on June 9. There was little discussion downstairs after the service.

The next page was blank. Steve entered the date, May 29, and began to write.

> Tonight's meeting of the steering committee was to make plans for closing the church. John was there to work with us. Instead, the committee reversed itself! They decided to keep going until the end of the year and began to talk about raising money. I raised the question about mission, and Sam replied, "We can't give to mission because we'll go under ourselves." I was to the point of crisis, and in a moment of heat I told them that was faithless to the point of blasphemy. It repudiates everything I've been preaching and trying to show. There

198

seems to be no mention of what God wants us to do, or how we can serve Christ. There's no sense of mission, even as a goal. How can I continue to pastor this congregation when I fundamentally disagree with their will and direction? They know I've been expecting to leave by the end of the year. Should I resign now? How do I bring the Word of God to these people?

Three Alternative Strategies

1. RAPID GROWTH CAMPAIGN

Desired result. Getting the word out about Reston Baptist.

Process. Media campaign—radio and TV spots plus large local newspaper ads. Aggressive door-to-door canvassing—laity under guidance of pastor. Begin with a one-mile radius from church plus every newcomer to Reston area. High public visibility of pastor—named presence at community events. All members take it upon themselves to invite friends/acquaintances to join them at worship.

Desired result. Creating favorable first impression of church.

Process. After-church greeters/introducers of visitors. Promote Sunday school. Visible display—pictures and description of church life and program.

Desired result. Incorporation of new members.

Process. Follow-up calls on all visitors—laity and pastor. Study/prayer/Bible-study groups of current members into which potential new members are incorporated. Ad hoc church groups/committees invite potential new members to join to increase their feeling of ownership of/commitment to Reston—missions, Sunday school, women's groups, etc.

Cost. Money for media campaign. Money for brochures about church life. Volunteered time for ad hoc evangelism steering committee (three to five persons plus pastor) to coordinate evangelism program; run and monitor media campaign; follow up new members, involving them in church life;

evaluate success of program. Additional volunteered time for study/prayer/Bible-study groups (at least two groups to start) and visitation/calling—given the urgency of the situation, most members will have to be involved in visitation training and visitation.

2. REORGANIZE UNDER SPECIAL SERVICE MINISTRY TO THE COMMUNITY

The primary ministry in such a reorganization would be a special service ministry to a community need. Such a ministry should be fundable in and of itself from individual laity, churches, and other organizations; there might be grant support in the first year or two, but eventually it would have to support itself. The ministry would employ a minister for, say, 90 percent of his/her time, the remaining 10 percent going to pulpit supply for the Reston congregation.

Examples of what this special ministry might be include: street ministry to youth, day care for elderly, media ministry to community, support ministry for young mothers, singles ministry, simplified-life-styles advocacy. The choice of this special ministry must grow out of a careful study of community needs and the possibility for funding.

Sample Budget

Total expenses: $30,000

Salary, fringe benefits, utilities for minister	$15,000
Housing allowance	6,000
Program	4,000
Reston church building maintenance/utilities	3,000
Reston church program	2,000

Total income: $30,000

Reston congregation pledges	$ 6,000
First Church in Wallaceboro contribution of parsonage	6,000
Building rental	2,000
Individual and church support of special service ministry	16,000

Non-financial costs to Reston members. (1) Run Reston's church life except for pulpit supply. (2) Constitute core board of directors for new ministry: (a) identify need and structure ministry to meet it; (b) generate ecumenical financial support, possibly also seeking funds from other private- and public-sector sources; (c) be willing to expand membership in and control of board of directors to incorporate persons from other supporting constituencies.

3. DISBAND WITH DIGNITY AND PURPOSE

Time span. 2 to 3 months.

Process. (1) Celebrate the goodness that was and the goodness that will be in a new form. (2) Grieve the goodness that has been lost. (3) Relocate current members in new church homes for continued nurture and expression of their Christian commitment: (a) identify variety of potential church homes; (b) allow for experimentation with variety of new church homes; (c) provide support and accountability structure which helps insure that persons will find a comfortable new location for their church life. (4) Possibly use lenten season with its symbolism of death and rebirth as appropriate time for this process.

Required. Commitment of a core group of current members to stick with the process and with one another during disbandment process and probably a few months beyond.

Some Questions for Analysis and Discussion

1. Should the pastor resign? Why?
2. Which of the three alternative strategies would you recommend? Can you think of other options open to the congregations?
3. What considerations about where to locate a new church and when to start it emerge from this case?
4. What might motivate members to more active participation in the church?

Note also the general questions on pages 28–29.

CASE STUDY D

A CHURCH NAMED LUCK

An Overview of the Case

This case study consists of excerpts from a larger report prepared by an outside consultant. The church asked the consultant to amass data that would help identify its strengths and weaknesses in preparation for some long-range planning. The case as reported here does not include the consultant's final recommendations. Data about the congregation were collected during a two-day visit to the congregation by the consultant.

Among the immediate financial decisions facing this congregation is what to do with a recently rediscovered endowment fund of $12,000. A previous pastor had invested the money in a mutual fund, and all track of it had been lost. In the parish council, strong arguments are being advanced for keeping it for anticipated major maintenance. Others say both principal and interest must be used for mission activities in the community, and that if the endowment is not so used, they will leave the church. No evidence survives of the donor's original wishes.

The long-range problems LUCK (the name is an acronym) faces are more serious. It has survived, by means of mergers, dramatic changes in its neighborhood. Now the congregation ponders which strategies are most helpful for it to pursue. LUCK's future hinges on three main concerns. In order of importance, these are: (1) the level of commitment of the members to LUCK and its ministry; (2) the number of members; and (3) the continued functional use of LUCK's building. Changes in any of these will have strong effects on LUCK's survival.

The situation faced by LUCK can be summarized using the outline in Diagram 2, page 79, as follows.

A. Present members are giving at a sacrificial level to support the church. Newer members cannot give at the same rate as older members who leave or die. Some discussions about how to recruit new constituencies has occurred, but no plans have been implemented.

B. No one knows if anyone has put LUCK in his or her will. There is debate in the church about whether the present endowment should be given for mission or saved for future maintenance. Some support from LUCK's three sponsoring denominations is possible.

C. The church has a reasonably effective budgeting system. The leaders have implemented such economizing measures as plastic storm windows.

D. There is general agreement about the purpose of the church. Members want LUCK to serve the needs of the community and to build a membership well equipped for that task. Among some of the older members there is a tendency to want to preserve the past, but not in ways narrowly limited to things as

they were, as was the case with St. John's Church
(Case A).
E. The key to this church's future is its constituency.
Who will be related to LUCK for purposes of worship and for providing services, and who for the purpose of being recipients of services? At present, the
two constituencies do not overlap.
F. The leadership is ready and able to begin making far-
reaching planning decisions.

Some Historical Perspectives

Forged from three predecessor congregations, the congregation whose name forms the acronym LUCK began its life
and ministry in June 1975. Merger resulted when a United
Methodist church and a United Presbyterian church implemented a plan of union titled "Merger for Mission." The
United Presbyterian church was itself a merger of two congregations. In 1974 the Presbyterian church was joined by a
predominantly black congregation that was affiliated with the
Southern Presbyterian denomination. The United Presbyterian and the Methodist congregations were predominantly
white. Today, LUCK continues its affiliation with three denominations.

All three predecessor congregations have distinguished histories, the stories of which have not been adequately preserved. In 1950 the United Presbyterian church had
membership numbering more than 2,100 and the United
Methodist church in excess of 3,400. The congregations offered   distinguished   leadership   in   their   respective
judicatories, boasted prominent pulpits, and undertook many
mission projects. By 1975, a quarter-century later, the United
Presbyterian church listed only 232 members, more than half
of whom had joined the year before as the result of the merger
with the black Presbyterian church. Moreover, the church
building, a strikingly attractive structure that still stands
empty, needed maintenance beyond the congregation's abil-

204

ity to provide. Six short blocks eastward, the United Methodist church had 247 members and a church building in reasonably good repair.

Plummeting membership had resulted in large part from drastic changes in the neighborhoods surrounding the congregations—from white to black, from middle and upper class to lower class, from moderate income to very low income. For well over a decade the neighborhood has housed many of the city's poorest residents. Changes came slowly but inexorably; membership declined every year from its peak in the early 1950s.

LUCK resulted, then, because bad times had befallen the three congregations. For 25 years the congregations had sustained deteriorating membership size, loss of purchasing power, and massive changes in the surrounding neighborhoods. Major changes would inevitably occur. Studies were commissioned, alternatives were considered, and eventually agreement to merge was reached. Almost defiantly, the congregations resolved to stay in their present community, even though many observers predicted failure and eventual disbanding of all the congregations or any merged congregation. None of the earlier studies had envisioned an interdenominational merger. Drawing, nevertheless, on a "spirit of unity and mutuality," according to "Merger for Mission," LUCK prepared to become "a new and innovative community-oriented church."

Today's membership in LUCK numbers 362, down from 440 in 1976 immediately following the merger (an annual decline of 2.96 percent). Because the surrounding community continues to deteriorate in property value and decrease in population, this continued decline in membership is not surprising. Many merged congregations, in fact, do not fare as well as LUCK. One sociologist's general rule is that a merged congregation tends to decline to the size of the larger of the uniting churches (in this case United Methodist church at 247) within five years. LUCK has done substantially better than this, notwithstanding reductions in the size of the pastoral staff from three full-time persons to one full-time and one part-time person.

In its seven years of existence, LUCK has led and participated in several ecumenical ministries and has sponsored community projects on its own. Notable among the cooperative efforts are United Ministries and the food pantry that LUCK houses. United Ministries, not to be confused with LUCK itself, at one time was sponsored by more than a dozen churches and groups, but closed its doors in October 1982 when sponsors dwindled in number and funding through denominations dried up. At its peak, United Ministries sponsored a "fresh-air" program that gave inner-city youth a week's summer vacation in Colorado, a methadone clinic for drug addicts, a well-baby clinic, a program to process complaints to city hall, and similar other efforts.

The food pantry, which provides groceries and staples to families in emergency situations, continues to offer this service out of the LUCK building. About 630 families encompassing 1,800 persons have received food from the pantry in 1982.

The invitation to the outside consultant to conduct a study of LUCK coincided, perhaps not accidentally, with the closing of United Ministries. An article in the local newspaper interpreted the closing as reflecting a general decline in the interest of whites in the inner city and the challenge of addressing human need there. The article went on to observe that ethnically white congregations have continued to leave the area in recent years. LUCK members, in this environment, again turned their attention to the persistent questions of the purpose of their ministry and the probability of their survival on the corner of Laurel and Orange streets.

According to one person contributing information for this study, a long-standing former Methodist member, the Methodist congregation began in 1902 on LUCK's present site in a large tent erected for the first service. The night before the first service, a storm blew the tent over, making a muddy shambles of what was to be a place of worship. Those worshipers who arrived at that first service decided to brave the unexpected cold weather, and the men, rolling up their pants legs, put the tent aright. The 1902 winds were neither as strong nor as sustained as the "winds" of the past quarter-century, but the "tent" has proven more durable. Members want to know, "How long will the storm last?" "How long can we stand against it?" "What can we do to mitigate the storm's effects on our community and our church?" "Will we be able to put the tent up again if it blows over?" These questions led to the commissioning of the study by the consultant.

Characteristics of the Community

The city's area-plan document for the community immediately surrounding the church says, "Some of the City's poorest people live in the area. . . . The housing units . . . are old, often in poor condition and expensive to maintain, rents and values are low." Income for families is about half what it is for the city as a whole. There are high vacancy and low owner occupancy rates. Uncertainty over the area's future has contributed to the structural conditions of the dwelling units being the poorest in the area. The racial breakdown is about 85 percent black, 12 percent white, and 3 percent other nonwhite. The average age of the population is much older than the city as a whole.

Interviews with city leaders indicate the future promises the same conditions as the recent past. There are no plans for the area except for it to continue to house the very lowest-income people in the city and for dwellings to be demolished when they no longer serve this purpose. Two recent major changes in the immediate neighborhood of LUCK are the completion of the North-South Freeway and the demolition of the Catholic hospital building in the next block. The full impact of these two changes has not yet been felt. Plans to build

207

a shopping center on the former site of the Catholic hospital appear to be at best uncertain.

In the larger area surrounding LUCK, a three-mile radius, there are many planning areas that have large tracts of land and many dwellings housing the city's poorest people. Other comparatively more stable communities may also be found. These tend to house young, upwardly mobile families, lower-middle-income families, and elderly families. The three-mile circle also includes the downtown business area and some communities with large, attractive older homes that are in the process of being renovated ("gentrification"), but these latter are in the vast minority.

TABLE D-1

Neighborhood Population Characteristics in One-mile and Three-mile Circles Around LUCK, 1970 and 1980

	THREE-MILE RADIUS			ONE-MILE RADIUS
	1970	1980	Annual Rate of Change (%)	1980
Total population	217,132	161,946	(−)2.54	30,652
Density (per square mile)	7,486	5,583	—	8,727
Population under 10 yrs. of age	35,242	21,799	(−)3.81	4,570
Population ages 10–19	37,216	24,902	(−)3.31	5,726
Population ages 20–34	45,365	45,705	0.01	6,337
Population ages 35–44	21,529	13,710	(−)3.63	2,307
Population ages 45–64	44,529	31,198	(−)2.99	7,005
Population over 64 yrs. of age	33,351	24,622	(−)2.61	4,707
Housing units	95,844	79,605	(−)1.69	13,101
Vacancy rate (%)	11.56	13.75	—	16.5
Area (square miles)	29.0	—	—	3.5

SOURCE: Research Data Center, Mid-America Regional Council

Table D-1 presents 1970 and 1980 census data for the one- and three-mile-radius circles around LUCK. The population has declined steadily during the past decade in all age groups, except for persons aged 20 to 34 years. This young-adult group has stayed about the same size, owing probably to the availability of low-cost housing for persons just starting in the work force. Overall, the population has declined at a rate of 2.54 percent per year. If this rate continues, by 1990 the population will be 134,000, and by 2000, it will be only a little more than 100,000. The age groups that are declining fastest are children under 10 years of age and adults aged 35 to 45, persons who would be the parents of the children. The number of older people is not declining quite so rapidly as most other age groups, but they too have left the area in significant numbers. The proportion of persons in each category is very similar for the one-mile- and the three-mile-radius circles, indicating there is not much difference in the age composition between the larger and smaller circles.

The proportion of vacant dwellings has increased over the past decade from 11.56 percent to 13.75 percent, reflecting the continued decline in housing quality and value. The vacancy rate is even higher in the one-mile circle around LUCK, with one dwelling in six being unoccupied.

Table D-2 lists the number of community facilities in the one- and three-mile circles around LUCK. Of particular interest is the number of churches, 45 within one mile and 191 within three miles. The one-mile circle has 12.1 percent of the three-mile circle's area, 18.9 percent of its population, 16.5 percent of its dwellings, but 23.6 percent of its churches. This may explain why some churches continue to leave the area. Churches have demonstrated their capacity to survive when most other community facilities have failed. Not unexpectedly, therefore, Table D-2 shows several ways in which the one-mile circle is lacking in community facilities. For example, it has no large parks, no shopping centers, no developing subdivisions (there is only one in the three-mile radius), no colleges, concert halls, or libraries. There are seven restaurants, only 4.3 percent of the total in the three-mile circle. People who need to eat out must leave the area.

209

Community Facilities in One-mile and Three-mile Circles Around LUCK, 1980

Type of Facilities	Three-mile Radius	One-mile Radius
Churches	191	45
Parks greater than 40 acres	2	0
Swimming pools	16	6
Shopping centers	11	0
Major office buildings	162	4
Art galleries	12	0
Hospitals	9	1
Developing subdivisions	1	0
Movies/Drive-ins	7	1
Restaurants	164	7
Concert halls	7	0
Colleges	6	0
Libraries	13	0
Apartment buildings	130	10
Subsidized housing	73	9
Industrial areas	12	1
Area (square miles)	29.0	3.5

In fact, the only community service where the facilities in the one-mile circle exceed proportionately that of the three-mile circle, besides churches, is in swimming pools—perhaps intended to cool off heated and potentially riotous summer crowds.

Some Characteristics of the Congregation's Membership

SIZE OF MEMBERSHIP AND FINANCIAL RESOURCES

The membership of LUCK and its predecessor congregations has declined much more rapidly than the neighborhood's population. As members died, became inactive, or transferred their memberships elsewhere, people moving into the community did not replace the members lost. Table

Membership, Attendance, and Total Income for LUCK and Predecessor Congregations: Selected Years, 1951–82

Year	Total Members	Average Attendance	Total Receipts	Deflated Receipts Per Member (1967 = 100)	Deflated Total Receipts (1967 = 100)
1982	362	140			
1981	372	146	$127,524	$130	$48,459
1980	386	160	131,620	143	55,280
1979	406	188	154,266	174	70,962
1978	442	210	150,528	174	77,070
1977	444		149,600	185	82,429
1976	440		149,572	199	87,798
1975[a]	479		158,126	202	96,773
1974[b]	447		113,330	202	90,398
1970	1,095		158,647	124	136,436
1965	1,714		—	—	—
1951	5,613		147,764	34	189,876

SOURCE: Church records

[a] Includes the black Presbyterian church.

[b] All data before this date do not include the black Presbyterian church.

D-3 charts this drastic decline; yet it was not so drastic as to kill the congregations.

Over the 30 years the congregation's income has remained about the same in actual dollars. When inflation is taken into account, however, LUCK is seen to have only one-fourth of the combined purchasing power of the United Methodist church and the United Presbyterian church in 1951.

Even so, today's members contribute substantially more per person than their 1951 counterparts did, even when inflation is taken into account. One member who qualifies for subsidized housing manages to contribute $40 per week. A high rate of giving among very dedicated members may often be found in churches in situations like LUCK's. Members perceive the importance of their financial contributions to the ministry and indeed the very life of the congregation.

211

Moreover, awareness of sacrificial giving on the part of some members encourages others to do the same.

NEW MEMBERS

Often important trends may be discovered by observing characteristics of new members. In the past four years, since the present pastor arrived, 30 people have joined LUCK. Of these, 24 are black and six are white. According to the pastor's recollection, 10 are the teenage children or foster children of members, 10 adults joined principally because of family ties to the church, and 10 joined principally because of the church's program or the geographic convenience of the church's location.

Over the next decade fewer teenage children of members will be joining the church, unless the church succeeds in attracting more young-adult members than it presently does. Similarly, the number of people who join because of family ties may be expected to decline because of the large number of church members who are single and live alone. LUCK's principal hope for growth is in the last of the above-mentioned categories: people who are attracted by the church's program and/or its location.

RACIAL COMPOSITION OF THE CONGREGATION

Of the 247 family units in LUCK, 76 or 30.8 percent are black and 169 or 68.4 percent are white. Two families are biracial. The 247 family units represent 362 persons, 114 of whom are black and 248 of whom are white. Black members tend to live closer to the church building and are somewhat younger than white members.

RESIDENCE LOCATION OF MEMBERS

The largest proportion of LUCK families (42.5 percent) live in the central part of the city no more than a five- to 10-minute drive from the church building. The next largest proportion of members, 28.7 percent, live in the southern part of the city, three to 12 miles away from the church building, while comparatively few families (4 percent) live equidistantly to the north within the city. About 17.8 percent live in suburban areas east and west of the city, and 6.5 percent live totally out of the region.

AGE OF MEMBERS

Slightly over 57 percent of the family heads are over 60 years old, while 34.3 percent are aged 40 to 60. The remaining 8.6 percent are under 40 years old. If the true median age were determined, which cannot be done from these rough estimates, it would be well over 60 years.

Black members are on the whole younger than white members, probably because many of the younger people who have joined the church recently are black. Older people are more likely to pledge to the church than are younger people, and are more likely to live alone.

The age distribution indicates that LUCK will be extensively involved in bereavement ministry over the next few years and will experience a significant loss of membership because of ill health and death of older members.

FAMILY SIZE

LUCK has a great number of members who live alone or are the only member of their household who holds membership. This is as true of black as of white members. Almost 70 percent live in households with no other LUCK members, and many of these may be presumed to live alone. Older people are the most likely to live alone, but also the younger members (under 40 years) are more likely than not to live in single-person households. Consequently the number of people who worship in family groups at LUCK is very small. This has important implications for the kinds of emphases and programs LUCK undertakes.

GIVING ACTIVITY IN LUCK

The largest proportion, 43.4 percent, of LUCK's members pledge regularly to the church's financial drives. Another 25.8 percent give regularly but do not pledge, leaving 30.7 percent who are inactive in the church's financial program. Obviously, some people who are mostly inactive in LUCK's services and programs do support the church financially. This is especially true of older people who live alone.

Characteristics of LUCK's Program and Ministry

WHY PEOPLE AFFILIATE WITH LUCK

When asked why they choose to be active in LUCK, members respond with comments about the character of the congregation, its purpose, and its ministry. Some say it is the deep appreciation people have for persons different from themselves that keeps them coming. Some simply call it love. One individual reflected, "We truly believe we are one people and God's children." Still another insists, "We're in the inner city to stay. We dream that this church will stay and serve." One individual seemed to summarize the opinions of others by saying, "God has placed us in this community and tells us to stay here. Eventually people will find our commitment inspiring and join us." Many of LUCK's members have moved beyond mere tolerance of each other's differences, through appreciation of these diversities, to the realization that they depend on these differences for their personal as well as congregational well-being.

In addition to comments such as these, the LUCK annual budget also reflects the congregation's priorities and, moreover, points to reasons why stalwart members have refused to abandon LUCK and why new members have joined. Except for the addition of sections on volunteers and on the internal financial operations, the six sections that follow correspond to the subdivisions of the 1982 LUCK budget.

PASTORAL LEADERSHIP

Although the merger agreement called for LUCK to continue a pastoral staff of three persons, one of whom was to be full time in community service ministries, in 1979 the pastoral staff was reduced to one full-time and one part-time person. The change was made ostensibly for financial reasons.

The present pastoral staff enjoys almost total support of the membership, with a great many of the persons interviewed giving high praise to their minister. Some say he is a key reason for their remaining with LUCK, and others compliment his down-to-earth style of leadership.

Originally, one pastor was to be supplied by each of the supporting judicatories. Now, with only one full-time pastor, the judicatories will take turns providing the head pastor. One of the consequences of this change is that LUCK might find itself without a pastor for an interim after a Methodist pastor is assigned elsewhere and before a Presbyterian pastor can be called. Several members are concerned about the negative effects of such an interim on LUCK. They wonder if a period of ambiguous pastoral leadership would unduly discourage LUCK members.

In 1982, 23.46 percent of the church's budget was given to pastoral support. Although this proportion is slightly lower than that of average Protestant churches, it may be expected to rise if salaries keep up with inflation and no further cuts are made in staff size.

WORSHIP SERVICE

LUCK's worship service continues the traditions of the predecessor congregations. Strong emphasis is placed on preaching that interprets the scriptures and Christian faith for everyday life. Members expect the sermons to be prophetic and challenging, while not ignoring the pastoral care of persons who need support and nurture. Strong emphasis is placed on the music program, which absorbs the largest part of the worship budget. In 1982, this amounted to 8.77 percent of the total budgeted expenses for LUCK. An active altar guild volunteers time to keep the sanctuary ready for worship.

BUILDING AND GROUNDS

LUCK's building provides approximately 28,000 square feet of space, far in excess of the needs of its present program. The sanctuary seats more than 500, and there is presently a need for only 200 to 250 seats. Some office space might be rented if suitable tenants could be found.

The building sustained a major fire in 1965, requiring a new roof and extensive repairs to the altar area of the sanctuary. As a result, LUCK is not now facing the major maintenance that would have been the case had the fire not occurred. Concern needs to be raised about the heating plant, however, especially the gas-fired boiler that heats the sanctuary. While it may last for many years, it could also become dysfunctional almost immediately. Plans for alternative sources of heat need to be developed.

A problem of undetermined cause has emerged in the basement under the sanctuary. The plaster ceiling above the particle-board suspended ceiling is crumbling and falling onto the suspended ceiling. The plaster may be giving way because of water soaking that occurred at the time of the fire, but there may be other causes. Some research into the source of the problem and possible remedies is warranted. The kitchen will require replacement of major appliances in the near future.

The educational wing is newer than the sanctuary, and is separated from it by fire doors. It has a separate chapel that could conceivably seat the entire congregation for worship on most Sundays should the sanctuary become unusable. The educational wing has a separate, newer heating system.

In general, LUCK's building is well maintained and attractive. It is a credit to its community and probably has helped to forestall rapid deterioration in the surrounding dwellings.

In 1982, 32.92 percent of the budget was allocated to building and grounds. A significant part of this, however, is a con-

216

tribution to the mission activities of the church, which require special maintenance and/or improvements in the building. The mission activities also place heavy burdens on the custodial staff.

MISSION PROGRAMS, BENEVOLENCE AND JUDICATORY SUPPORT

Although the mission budget represents only 1.78 percent of LUCK's total budget, community mission assumes a much larger importance than this. For the most part, this budget item includes only direct contributions to community service agencies such as Tracy House, Foster Families Ministries, a house for battered women, and some funds to meet direct emergencies.

Additionally, many LUCK members contribute money, food, and time in behalf of the church to support community-oriented mission activities. Especially notable is the food pantry mentioned earlier, which operates from the church office. LUCK pays benevolences to its parent denominations, which represent 9.64 percent of the total budget in 1982.

CHURCH SCHOOL, NURTURE, AND FELLOWSHIP

Only 4.38 percent of LUCK's budget goes for education, fellowship, and nurture, and this is largely expended for educational supplies and chancel flowers. The only paid person in the church school is a nursery attendant. Although there is far too much space for the current educational program, the rooms are attractive and inviting to serious inquiry. The volunteer teaching staff has high credentials and has high expectations of participants. Church schools have some modest funds of their own that are not part of the church budget.

Volunteers have developed a special program for the nurture of shut-ins.

OFFICE EXPENSES

On the surface, the 19.01 percent of the church budget that goes for office expense appears to be high. Yet the office staff also serves as staff for most of the mission concerns of the congregation. The office is efficiently run and orderly in appearance.

BUDGET PROCESSES AND FINANCE MANAGEMENT

The church leaders prepare the annual budget, which has in the past been reasonably predictive of actual expenses. The budget does not, however, predict or even list income. In recent years, the budget has been met by withdrawing funds from reserves, a practice that cannot continue when the principal of the endowment becomes eroded. Predictions of how expenses can be met need to be part of every church budget.

The market value and the investment policies related to the endowment funds are neither published nor well known by church leaders. The treasurer does not serve on the parish council. The same person counts the offerings and deposits the funds in the bank. In effect, the financial secretary and treasurer functions are carried by the same person. The present treasurer received the books unaudited and in bits and pieces. At present no one who handles church money is bonded, and there is no regular independent audit of the church books. While there is absolutely no evidence of poor handling of funds on the part of anyone, these precautionary measures are well advised in every church.

The treasurer has recently implemented a voucher system for paying bills, which appears to be functioning well.

VOLUNTEERS

LUCK has reason to be proud of the number of volunteers it has, the quality of their work, and their dedication to the purposes of the congregation. There is a service auxiliary that makes handcrafted items for sale to benefit community service agencies and a volunteer's guild that responds to needs identified by the pastoral and office staffs. The adult church-school classes also contribute volunteer time and funds to community mission projects.

Summary of LUCK's Strengths, and Some Related Concerns and Issues That Require Attention

1. Luck's Strengths
   a. A dedicated core of members resolutely determined to stay in the inner city.
   b. A wide range of skills and abilities volunteered by LUCK members, many of whom see their involvement in LUCK as a lay ministry.
   c. The endowment fund, which provides some ongoing support of present programs and is probably large enough to finance one major maintenance project, such as the heating system.
   d. LUCK's location at Laurel and Orange, which provides ready access to persons in extreme need.
   e. LUCK's previous failures, which are leading through sometimes painful reassessments toward more realistic goals and more manageable means of accomplishing the goals.
   f. LUCK's pastoral staff and the popular support it enjoys among the membership.
   g. LUCK's building, which is well maintained and attractive.
   h. The interracial, multidenominational composition of the membership, which, although not unique, provides a demonstration of the benefits of diversity in a congregation.
   i. The two-building combination, which would allow all LUCK's programs to continue in one or the other building should either become unusable.
   j. LUCK members' concern for the people of the community, which does not require these people to be active in the church or have other "strings" attached.
   k. LUCK's support network to other churches, which helps it channel food and other services to poor people.
   l. LUCK's model maintenance practices—for example, the recent installation of Plexiglas storm windows for saving energy.

2. Some Concerns
   a. LUCK needs bonding for all people who handle church money and a regular audit of church books. Attention should be given to the other concerns for sound fiscal management practices identified above.
   b. The endowment should be monitored more carefully and aggressively in order to produce greater growth and income from interest. (Some churches and educational institutions are having success with selling stock options as a conservative and responsible way of producing growth of investment funds.)
   c. A plan needs to be developed in the event of failure of the heating plant either to replace it or to leave one of the two buildings unheated during the colder months.
   d. The rolls should be cleaned, and minimum expectations of members should be set.
   e. LUCK has not succeeded in attracting many new members who share the present members' vision and mission. Moreover, very little effort is made to evangelize or attract new members.
   f. LUCK receives only modest support from judicatories for its ministries, and judicatory officials are not clear about how they can be helpful to LUCK. Communication between judicatories about LUCK is not good.
   g. There is little contact of LUCK members with the needy of the community that is not connected directly to the giving and receiving of services. There are too few cooperative efforts in determining what needs the church is best able to address.
   h. LUCK lacks a deferred giving program that encourages older members to leave part of their estates to the congregation.
   i. The histories of LUCK and its predecessor congregations have not been preserved. Some of the older members have historical materials that should be assembled.
   j. LUCK members fear the fact that many of their number are reaching advanced ages and experience this as a threat rather than an opportunity.

k. LUCK lacks an overall strategy to inform its decisions about the future. Inordinate concern for meeting immediate needs is tending to replace long-range planning.

Some Questions for Analysis and Discussion

1. What long-range plans would you recommend to LUCK?

2. Suppose the dishwasher broke down and a new replacement would cost $7,000. A rebuilt model would cost $3,500. A dishwasher could be employed at $4.50 per hour. What decision would you advocate to the LUCK trustees?

3. If the members of LUCK decided to try to hold on to their building until such time as people start to move into the neighborhood again, what strategies should they follow?

4. If the members of LUCK decided to expand their mission expenses in the hope that people outside LUCK would see their good works and support them, what strategies should they follow?

5. If the members of LUCK decided to start a neighborhood renaissance to stimulate community renewal, what strategies should they follow?

See also the general discussion questions listed on pages 28–29.

CASE STUDY E

EDENVILLE UNITED METHODIST CHURCH*

An Overview of the Case

Like LUCK, Edenville is faced with the familiar dilemma:
should it put money into building or into programs and personnel? Unlike LUCK, however, the church has no strong
sense of direction to guide its decisions. It has some discretionary funds—that is, money it will have to decide how to
spend—and clearly the decision about how to spend them will
have great impact on the future well-being of the congregation.

There are structural problems with the comparatively new
building, a not uncommon situation. Many churches built in
the 1950s and 1960s have structural defects that are only now
beginning to show. This is especially true of various modern

*This case was prepared by George E. Schreckengost, as-
sociate director, East Ohio Conference Council on Ministries, as a basis for discussion rather than to illustrate
effective or ineffective handling of a situation.

architectural experiments that have failed to provide long-lasting structural soundness.

Edenville needs to pay particular attention to the investment strategy of its building fund. Left at 5¼ percent or even in certificates of deposit, the value of the principal is likely to be eroded by inflation.

Using the categories of Diagram 2, page 79, Edenville's situation may be described as follows.

A. Motivation to give among existing members could be increased, and there is still some possibility of increasing the number of members.
B. Edenville is probably at the point where it should begin laying the groundwork for bequests, wills, and major gifts. It has already received one such gift.
C. The preparation of the church budget is confused because its members are not clear which strategy will lead to the long-range results they want. Will improving the building bring more money for program by increasing membership, or will more program bring in the people to provide support for improving the building? As a result of this confusion, not only the budget but also plans for capital expenses are left undecided.
D. The congregation's goals are to have both a satisfactory building and an effective church program of worship, service, and training—the kind of desired result common to a great many congregations.
E. As written, the case is not explicit about the demographic changes occurring in Edenville, and it shows to some extent the problems of doing planning without such information.
F. There are many points at which changes could be made at Edenville, but the most critical one is strategy about which resources will best accomplish the church's desired results: building first or program first.

Edenville United Methodist Church

As they walked to the parking lot, Jerry Young asked Phil Baker, "What do you think the chances are that the administrative board will adopt our recommendation?"

Phil paused a moment before he responded. "I'm not overconfident, but I think the vote will be in our favor. The members can't help but see the strain the pastor is showing from carrying the pastoral load alone."

The men had just left a meeting of the staff-parish relations committee of the Edenville United Methodist Church. Jerry and Phil were discussing the action taken in the meeting—to recommend that the church hire a youth minister on a half-time basis. Phil had been a leader in the church for several years and was usually aware of how members felt about decisions being considered by the board. On this issue, however, he was uneasy about what to expect. He reflected, "Six years ago the church dealt with a similar type of recommendation. It was approved, but people disagreed whether it produced the results they wanted. Also, there are a few other factors that may affect the board members' reactions."

"During the past 10 years," Phil continued, "the people in our church have been perplexed by several unexpected developments. Think about them: We'd been experiencing phenomenal growth in the church and the area, but that suddenly stopped. In fact, we've fallen back from where we were then. When you take count, you'll also recall that we've had five ministers during this decade, with four changes in the pastoral arrangements."

"Then the plans for the new worship unit and other rooms were shelved," Jerry added. "We've bought two parsonages, and now the trustees are recommending that we sell the second one. And financially it's been like riding a roller coaster! Some people may vote against this simply to avoid another change."

The City of Edenville

Edenville is an incorporated community located in the urban fringe of two metropolitan areas. It had 4,060 residents in 1960 and 6,375 in 1970. The population in 1980 is estimated between 7,500 and 8,000. Primarily a "bedroom" community, Edenville has a limited amount of small businesses and light industry. Economically, it is upper-middle class. The 1970 median family income of $13,250 was sixth highest of all communities in Chippewa County.

During the 1960s the community grew rapidly in response to highway improvements and the development of businesses and industries in nearby areas. There are more than 50 cities and villages within a 15-mile radius of Edenville, many of which are easily accessible by good arterial highways. The slowdown of the building boom of the Northeast and North Central regions of the country was also felt here. The decline in housing starts and a drop in the birth rate combined to retard population growth and effectively to delay plans for additional business development.

The churches were also affected, especially mainline churches. A Disciples of Christ church expanded its facilities, but did not grow as expected. Attempts to start a Reformed church had little success, and the Synod withdrew its mission pastor. An Episcopal mission failed to establish an adequate footing, and soon had to share a rector with a congregation in another community. The United Methodist church's rapid growth halted abruptly.

Several new houses have been built at the decade's end, but the pace is slow. Cutbacks in production and personnel layoffs by several major industries add to the already negative impact of a tight money market on further development of this community at the present time.

Changes in the Church

Jerry Young was disturbed by Phil Baker's fear that changes during the past 10 years might weaken the vote favoring a part-time youth minister. He remembered the facts that convinced him a youth minister was needed. A profile of the church membership had been made public, for one thing, and it showed that the church had more members over 65 than it had under 20. Ned Caldwell, the church school superintendent, had observed, "There isn't much variation in the number of members we have in any 10-year age grouping from any other 10-year age group. That's not a healthy sign for a church. In fact, the median age of our membership is in the 40 to 44 age bracket, which is somewhat high. Yet a little over one-fourth of our Sunday-school enrollment is made up of junior-high and senior-high youth. We need someone to work closely with our youth and leaders to get more of these young people to become active church members!"

The question in Jerry's mind was not about the need for the youth minister; he was convinced thoroughly of that. But he wondered if half-time help for the minister would really be enough. Phil Baker's comment about the strain showing on the pastor was serious. The church had had two full-time pastors for the four and a half years until this summer. Since July 1 Roscoe Berwell had tried to keep up the work previously done by two people. He was also an active leader in the Conference, which must be an added drag, thought Jerry. "The board *has* to approve our request!" he exclaimed to himself.

If Jerry Young and Phil Baker (and the staff-parish relations committee) feel so strongly about the need to add staff, why should these factors Phil recounted seem so important to the vote? What happened in the 1970s?

MEMBERSHIP AND ATTENDANCE TRENDS

The Methodist Church in Edenville was started at the close of the Civil War. It was a small church until Edenville's growth began in the mid-1950s. From 1955 to 1965 the church membership increased from 248 to 861. In 1960 the congregation relocated in a new building. The new facilities were modest but attractive, and they made program expansion possible. Average Sunday-school attendance peaked at 315 in 1968; membership and worship attendance peaked in

1970 with 1,098 members and an average of 450 in worship. The facilities were overcrowded.

Then a decline in membership and worship attendance followed the drop in Sunday-school attendance that had begun two years earlier. This decrease also coincided with a change in pastors. In 1980 the average attendance at worship has been 288; the Sunday-school average has been 141. The current membership is 949.

PASTORAL STAFF

Through 1974 Edenville was typically served by one pastor. Late that year the leadership considered a request similar to the recommendation now being made by the staff-parish relations committee—to add a half-time pastor. The decision was affirmative, so in 1975 Pastor Harold Wiseman's ministry was supplemented half-time by Pastor Frank Runyon. With an agreement that the two men would serve as co-pastors, Runyon was appointed full time in January 1976. Harold Wiseman accepted an appointment to another church in 1977, so the church reevaluated the co-pastorate pattern. The result was the appointment of Frank Runyon as senior minister and Barry York as associate minister. In 1980 both Runyon and York left for new appointments, and Roscoe Berwell came as Edenville's lone pastor.

Shortly after Harold Wiseman came to Edenville in 1971, he became concerned about the future quality of relationships within the congregation. He asked a church planner, "Can a church with 1,200 or more members maintain any real relationships as a community? Or can quality church relationships be maintained best if we urge some of our people to become the nucleus in starting a new congregation a few miles away?" Following such inquiries, Harold concluded that he should work toward strengthening the life of small groups in the Edenville church so that everyone in the congregation could really "belong."

By 1974 Harold determined that he needed help from

227

someone with special skills for developing small-group life. Frank Runyon recalls, "When Harold talked to me about this, he said he would like me to develop the relational dimension through a care program and retreats. In the interviews with Edenville committees some questions were asked about my work with youth. Youth work was not one of my strengths, and I thought it was agreed that my primary task was to develop the interrelational life within the congregation, especially among adults." Periodically during his tenure at Edenville, however, Frank would hear that several persons had understood he would be the youth worker they had wanted. Their disappointment is known by lay leader Phil Baker, who hopes the expectations will be clearer this time if the church approves the proposal to hire a youth minister.

CHURCH PROPERTIES

The first of the two parsonages purchased during the decade resulted from trustee concerns about the potential risk for parsonage children in case of fire in the former parsonage. In 1971, shortly after Harold Wiseman became pastor, a much more adequate house on the same street was found at an excellent price.

A possible second parsonage was discussed in 1977 as a residence for Frank Runyon. Until then the Runyons commuted from their home near Pine Hill, where he also served half-time. A family gave $10,000 for the down payment, but the trustees were very reluctant to assume responsibility for a second parsonage. With assurance that the Runyons planned to serve at Edenville for at least a few years, the trustees made the purchase. Before the Runyons were to move, however, Harold Wiseman announced that he was leaving. The Runyons therefore moved into the "main" parsonage, and the new associate's family became the occupants of the newly-purchased house.

Limited by a sanctuary that seats 230 persons, the church

provided duplicate worship services on Sunday mornings. The needs for additional space for fellowship events, classrooms, and staff could not be as easily accommodated. Plans were developed for a new wing with classrooms, a larger sanctuary, a narthex, a choir room, and offices. The architects delivered the preliminary drawings and model in 1975. That fall the administrative board voted to make financial development the major 1976 priority in order to support the full-time co-pastor and to raise the additional $206,000 required for breaking ground for phases 1 and 2 of the building plans. That would provide all the designed facilities except the new sanctuary.

Less than a third of the building-fund goal was reached in pledges. Groundbreaking was postponed. When it became obvious that receipts for the building fund were far short of the amount pledged, it was decided to shelve the program indefinitely. Several persons were quite disappointed, but many also expressed relief in light of the community's population trends.

Extensive repairs have been needed in the church building. In 1980 the sanctuary's gable roof was reshingled and the heating system was replaced. The flat roof over the rest of the building leaks badly. As trustee Bill Myers puts it, "All this attention going toward staff, parsonages, missions, and a possible addition distracted us from the fact that parts of this building were going to pot! Maintenance and repair must become a new priority around here, or we won't have a place fit for people to come. That flat roof needs to be redesigned or rebuilt. It will never be right the way it is."

FINANCES

Concurrent with the tapering off of membership and attendance, Edenville has been confronted with dramatic increases in expenses. The treasurer's reports show such major changes as these: 1980 fuel costs, 227% increase over 1970;

1980 electricity costs, 252% increase over 1970; 1980 denominational askings, 142% increase over 1970; 1980 total expenditures, 142% increase over 1970.

The pace of rising costs and the income picture in 1977 led the finance committee to project a considerable deficit for the year. The purchase of the second parsonage and the lower payment of building-fund pledges added to the committee's pessimism. Some finance committee members expressed the opinion that the committee should make the decisions on anything related to finances. But a concept was being discussed that would change the financial priorities.

The idea surfaced at a fall planning retreat. Sam Pence remembers the event. "Some members were convinced that a drastic step was needed to put things on a firmer footing. We talked about the promotion of tithing, or at least of members contributing a definite portion of their income," he recalls. "The Bible not only talks about the giving of our 'first fruits' as a tithe, but it also speaks of our being the example of 'first fruits.' So we decided that the church can best demonstrate the principle by tithing the income the church receives."

Frank Runyon, pastor at that time, explained the action to a friend. "The first 10 percent of all undesignated receipts goes first to World Service and Conference benevolences as soon as receipts are in at the end of the month. When that appointment has been paid in full, the tithe could go to anything that is not a bill of the local church. And remember, the people consider the Conference operating apportionment to be a local church obligation, not a fund eligible for its 'First Fruits' gifts."

Adopted by a sizeable majority, the First Fruits Program was implemented immediately. By year's end the projected deficit was overcome, and the church, for the first time, began sending monthly payments to the conference treasurer. Although strongly supported by local leaders, the program has not caught on with the majority of members. Fifty-five percent of the giving units still give a dollar or less per week as an average. Nevertheless, the 1980 weekly receipts for the church budget average $2.90 per member, which equals $9.50 per worshiper. Sam Pence testifies, "Since our church started to give a minimum of its first 10 percent of nondesignated receipts to World Service and benevolences, our needs have been taken care of by sufficient receipts."

ATTITUDES AFFECTING THE DECISION

Past experience indicates that conflicting opinions will be vigorously expressed. Some persons may resist the recommendations for hiring a youth minister and selling a parsonage due to objections they had to previous actions by the board or committees. These differences among Edenville members, however, are generally counterbalanced by a common commitment to maintain and strengthen the sense of Christian community, of being a family-type fellowship.

Several members reflect a feeling that Edenville's "bubble has burst." The optimism of the 1960s has been tempered by the changing trends of the 1970s. This has led to some confusion about priorities. Some business executives in the church interpret the First Fruits Program as a decision to depart from sound business practices, and expect the church's future to be further threatened by actions strongly supported by those who advocate "launching out by faith." The finance chairperson hopes to bridge those differences. He says, "I sincerely believe that when you tell and show the members the financial position of the church and explain that the church is them, each and every one, all for one, one for all, you get the necessary support. It is essential to get all the necessary facts on the table if we are to make sound decisions; then we share the needed information with the congregation so they will understand and support what we decide to do."

Among the Unmade Decisions

There is much more to be decided by the Edenville United Methodist Church than a simple recommendation to hire a half-time youth minister. How would you help the administrative board decide:

1. Should the church hire a youth minister half-time?
   a. Some feel the funds should be used for maintenance, not staff.
   b. Many consider the needs of the youth program to be crucial at this time.
   c. Some think a full-time associate minister or Christian-education staff person should be hired, with youth work being one of his/her major responsibilities.
   d. The congregation was divided when it acquired a second pastor in 1975.
2. Should the church sell or retain the second parsonage?
   a. It is currently occupied by a renter.
   b. Several persons are disturbed that the parsonage is in an adjacent community.
   c. Some think the church should have another resident staff member who could live in the house.
   d. Several feel the church should not have a second parsonage.
   e. Some want the parsonage to be sold and the money used for building repair or expansion.
3. How should the church balance the desires for repair of the present building and for building an addition?
   a. There is general agreement that the flat roof over the classrooms must be fixed soon.
   b. No careful study has been made of redesign possibilities of the present classrooms, although investigation showed that the joists would not support any addition above the present classrooms.
   c. Additional fellowship space is considered by many to be a need as important as new classrooms. Such space is now limited to the sanctuary overflow area and a parlor-classroom.
   d. The building-fund balance, although not regularly reported, is estimated to be about $100,000.

Some Questions for Analysis and Discussion

1. How would you advise Edenville on the three unresolved questions at the conclusion of the case?
2. What would be the implications for this church if attendance at worship continued to drop to 200?
3. What strategy would you suggest for increasing contributions of present members and for increasing optimistic views of the church's future?

See also the general discussion questions on pages 28–29.

CASE STUDY F

A NEW CHURCH
FOR NEWARK*

An Overview of the Case

In order to call their first full-time pastor, the people who organized what was to become a congregation called The New Ark in a small city named Newark prepared a proposal asking their sponsoring denomination, the United Church of Christ, for $39,000. The grant was to be paid over a three-year period to help underwrite part of the expense for the employment of a full-time organizing pastor. This case is made up of edited excerpts from their proposal. A brief description of their situation in 1983, the fourth year of The New Ark's existence, concludes the case study.

*This case was prepared by the founding members of The New Ark Church and is included here as a basis for discussion.

234

At the time the proposal was written The New Ark had no budget, no building, and no organizational structure. It did not even have a name. There were only 30 families, a part-time temporary pastor, and an agreement with another church to allow Sunday-evening meetings in its building for six months. Basic financial decisions had to be made about such questions as how to house the congregation, how to go about employing a pastor, what should be the extent of local church programming, what would be the mission commitment of the congregation, and how the new church would go about soliciting funds from prospective members and subsidies from the denomination.

The church's financial circumstances can be summarized using categories from Diagram 2, page 79, as follows.

A. The New Ark has no history of how to solicit contributions from members, no etiquettes or taboos to limit them. Some of the founding members have been putting personal money aside so that when the church gets underway, they will make a sizeable lump-sum contribution.

B. While the church is not likely to get money from a bequest in the near future, it can expect to get some denominational subsidy to get started. The founding members see this as a loan, which they will repay as a moral obligation.

C. The church is not yet clear what resources it will need to acquire to accomplish its ministry. Does it need a building or can it share a building with an existing congregation? Does it need a full-time pastor, or can trained lay volunteers provide counseling, worship leading, teaching, preaching, and other roles traditionally filled by clergy? Does it need denominational hymnals?

D. Its purpose is reasonably clear. Its members wish to create a church with a strong Christian social ministry, with innovative and widely participatory worship services, and with a strong family emphasis.

E. The original constituency of this church comprises three groups: members of an experimental ecumenical church that failed and for which the members are still grieving; former members of a large church in the community, who left because they perceived the large church was too traditional and unimaginative; and people who were not affiliated with any church in Newark. At present the concerns of the first two groups are primary. Over time, the third group will predominate.

F. Decisions at all the points on Diagram 2 apply to this church. It has able, aggressive leaders who are waiting impatiently to get on with the tasks.

The proposal to the denomination for funds that follows in part below begins with a description of the prospective members as they were in the summer of 1979.

1. Who Are the Prospective Members? What Are We About?

We number 30 families with 82 persons. The demographic profile of this nucleus is slightly lower in number of single persons and higher in number of professionals than the general community. Of those now on the mailing list, 80 percent are families with parents aged 30 to 50 and 1 to 3 children, 10 percent are single people primarily of college age, and 10 percent are families with parents aged over 50 whose children are grown. About half the adults are scientists, engineers, or skilled workers. A fourth are associated with the university or education. Another fourth are associated with city businesses and government. The commonality of values in mission and Christian family life is probably greater than these statistical data might indicate.

Roughly one-third of the congregation is drawn from the former Glasgow Ecumenical Ministry (a cooperative Presbyterian, Methodist, and Episcopal mission). This mission, begun in 1971 in the Glasgow area south of Newark, expected to reach people in new housing developments that never materialized. The congregation instead drew people interested in informal, creative worship and in possibilities of transcending denominational boundaries. This spring, the Glasgow congregation voted to join the effort to develop a new congregation.

236

A second third of the congregation is drawn from a Presbyterian background. During the 1970s, a group with an informal, intergenerational, participatory worship style grew in a large United Presbyterian church. This worship style attracted 150 to 200 participants per Sunday over a four-year period, many of whom would not have attended services with more traditional worship forms. The parent organization reconsolidated to a more traditional style during 1978, a plan that was consistent with its large building, a staff with one pastor, and the more-than-800-member congregation.

The potential charter members are seriously working to unite these two groups and are actively seeking new church members. The remaining one-third of the presently interested people are from United Church of Christ backgrounds or have responded to a newspaper advertising campaign.

During August and thereafter, we began to list and share our visions as a first step toward developing a covenant of our life together. Because of our diversity, our commitment to consensus, and our open discussion of issues, we decided that comments elicited for the purpose of shaping this report be included. By doing this, we hope the readers of this proposal will catch something of the spirit of our fledgling church.

A. Understandings of the Nature of the Church

—The church is caring concern. It encourages respect for individuality and individual rights. The Christian community gives without expecting something in return. And, therefore, it is a community built on love for God, for one another, for the world, and for ourselves.

—A church must worship together in the communion of bread and wine, as well as in other ways. It must be doing works for others because of Christ. We are acknowledging "divinity" in ourselves—the potential to do great things—just as the early church did.

—We believe in Christ as our Savior. We have a mission: to spread the Good News, to serve the broader community, and to seek out areas of injustice and work to correct them.

—Our church will be a place to come if you are lonely.

—We will become a People of the Covenant, based on our traditions and our present perception of who we are in order to express willingness to accept and respond to the gift that was Christ. We share our talents as well as our hurts and weaknesses. That enables our community to become the royal priesthood whose members minister to one another in the name of Christ.

B. Our Expectations of Worship

—Participation by the congregation in planning worship and during worship itself is essential. Worship should be experiential rather than passive or merely intellectual.

—Worship should be intergenerational, with children and all ages of adults involved in all parts. Worship is not something done *to* the people but an experience *of* and *by* the people—planned by them, led by them, and so on. The children need to be obviously involved throughout the service, not paraded in just for a children's sermon and then shuttled off to some classroom.

—The church will have nontraditional styles of worship that emphasize total congregational involvement and that seek new ways to be family oriented, but that always evolve from scripture as the central focus.

—Planning worship should be a joint effort among lay people, with the role of the pastor being only advisory.

—Worship will try to capture in the liturgy the Good News so that there can be physical participation of all people.

—Worship will have theological depth sufficient to satisfy adult needs of faith and personal growth, and will be creative enough in its presentation to keep younger worshipers involved.

C. The Mission Concerns of the Emerging Church

—We should show by example the blessings of Jesus Christ, sharing the needs of our community.

—We need to be caring for ourselves and caring for the greater community. Time and money will be given generously outside the church.

—Social action and mission outreach will be very important, with 30 to 50 percent of resources given to this cause.

—We will need to make tangible efforts to seek out opportunities to help others; we will not wait for people to come to us.

—The mission of the church is for reconciliation, for justice, for shalom, and for other people, with no strings attached.

—Mission should include personal, global involvement of members in issues of justice.

—We have a mission to and with the university students living in our city.

—We need to learn how to be the benefactors of the mission of others—for example, to seek from Third-World people their perception of the Good News.

D. The Quality of Our Life Together

—We will have generosity and gentleness toward each other as we learn, grow, and make mistakes.

—We hope that attitudes of support and encouragement for one another will emerge even as we disagree and struggle together, and that people will be enthusiastic about one another's interests and expressions even when they are not one's own.

—We want to reach out to people who are different from us: ethnically, in level of education, in life-style, in sexual orientation.

—Our church will be a place where we become equipped to cope with our lives and to use those lives in activities that glorify God and acknowledge that we are God's children.

—We want to be a place to grow, to know, to become—and a caring community to surround and support that activity.

E. A Major Mission Emphasis to Unchurched People

—We will appeal to those who are looking for a caring community they have not found in other established churches.

—Many young, single people who feel out of place in

what is too often a couple-oriented religious situation will find a welcome here.

—Our church will be different enough from presently existing, mainly conservative churches so as to attract people who have either been turned off by religion or who have not tried religion.

—We have a mission especially to the nonchurched and the committed who have found other institutional churches unsatisfactory.

2. What Designs Have Been Developed for Program and Mission?

We have good reason to believe that the proposed mission and method will work. A majority of our present adults have spent some time unchurched: we spent periods in which our values and cosmology outgrew our more narrow definition of theology. During the past 15 years, we have rejoined the active church in settings that we often characterize as "alternatives." For the majority, informal worship has been the norm for an average of five years. A major part of this nucleus consists of people drawn from two prior pilot programs.

The polity of our life is congregationally based. Several committees in functional areas defined by the congregation are operating. Their meetings are open to any who attend. Their activities are coordinated by a committee whose six members are selected by lot from those willing to serve for six-month terms. Decisions are by consensus. We anticipate writing bylaws in the fall; our current methods are intended to maintain maximum flexibility as we develop an open, congregational style. We have begun a church school with six age-level classes from preschool through adult.

Worship is planned in monthly blocks by groups of four or five lay people who form a study group guided by the pastor. After a month's study, the group then plans and carries out the succeeding month's worship in consultation with the pastor. At all times lay participation in leadership of the liturgy and congregational involvement in the acting out of the worship is a high priority. Most services contain a segment in which the children gather and contribute orally and physically to the theme of the day's worship. In response to the diversity of custom, communion is offered in both wine and grape juice and is celebrated once a month.

3. How Will the Congregation Be Housed?

Rental of space has proved adequate for 1979. The Unitarian Fellowship building has been appropriate for worship and Christian education, with some adaptation of our hours to their available times. For 1980, we anticipate continued use of the Unitarian Fellowship Center on Sunday evening, and use of the George Wilson Community Center or perhaps the Masonic Hall on Sunday morning.

For long-term facilities needs, several possibilities are being explored:

a. sharing facilities with another church
b. renting separate spaces for worship, office, and so on, in commercial facilities
c. building joint facilities with a weekday community service
d. building or purchasing our own facility

If these facilities can be adapted from available buildings, then costs will be reduced. If our own building must be built, then the land will cost roughly $100,000 and the initial building unit roughly $250,000 in 1979 dollars. For this expenditure, we would need massive underwritten loans.

Our prior experience with facilities has been at two poles. The Glasgow ministry had difficulty maintaining focus without some physical location. The large, multimillion-dollar buildings many of us have served in have also inhibited church programs. Many of us have also had experience with multifunctional facilities. Our desire is that any facility used for worship by the congregation also have a broader mission for the Newark community.

The New Ark Proposed Budget, Extending to 1983

EXPENSES	(half year) 1979	1980	1981	1982	1983
Pastor	$3,000	$23,500	$25,000	$28,000	$31,000
Staff, part-time secretary	—	—	3,000	6,000	6,600
Facilities	2,300	6,000	6,600	7,200	8,000
Operating supplies	1,000	4,000	5,000	6,000	6,000
Conference	—	1,000	1,800	2,500	3,000
Benevolences	500	3,500	4,000	5,000	6,000
Outreach/Publicity	300	2,000	3,000	2,500	2,400
	7,100	40,000	48,400	57,200	63,000
INCOME					
Local	7,800	20,000	35,400	51,200	63,000
Denominational support	-0-	20,000	13,000	6,000	-0-
No. giving units	30	38	60	80	90
Avg. $/Unit (per year)	520	525	590	640	700

4. Financing the New Church

During 1979, we have balanced giving and expenditures. The total budget [shown in Table F-1] is based on the $300 per week average contribution of July and August from 30 families.

The 1980 and 1981 budgets are based on 10 percent increases from the base $600 per year per family average projected for 1979 and 50 percent per year increases in the number of giving units over the first two years.

Under the circumstances, it seems impractical to employ an organizing pastor on a full-time basis without the assistance of the denomination. We ask for 50 percent financing in the first year ($20,000 in 1980) and 27 percent in the second year ($13,000 in 1981), and 10 percent in the third year ($6,000 in 1982).

An Update on The New Ark

The remainder of the original proposal consists of a lengthy description of Newark and environs. It is a moderately wealthy city of about 50,000 residents, 58.1 percent of whom live in their own homes. Students at the state university make up 13.6 percent of the population. About 45 percent of the population is under 25 years old, and only 8 percent are over 65 years. Most of the homes have been built since 1960, and over a third of the people are college graduates. A third of the work force is professional. The population has grown 25 percent over the past 10 years. The churches of Newark, many of which trace their origins to the eighteenth century, are basically traditional in approach, and some of them are very fundamentalistic.

The New Ark developed a statement of mission that found its first expression as a diagram, an open circle. Its mandala-like design reflects its members' concerns for service to the world, reconciliation, group ministries, and openness to people of different orientations. They employed their first full-time pastor in 1981, a year later than planned. Their budgets have been very close to the initial projections. They have relied more heavily on denominational subsidy, however, than they expected they would—$54,000 through 1983.

| | TOTAL EXPENSES | |
	ACTUAL	PROJECTED
1981	$39,350	$48,400
1982	55,200	57,200
1983 (budgeted)	66,500	63,000

The congregation is presently meeting in the basement of a Baptist church. There are seats and benches for 90 people, and there is standing-room only for most services.

Some Questions for Analysis and Discussion

1. What would you say the chances for The New Ark's long-term survival are? Why?

2. What strategies would you recommend to the church for

243

such financial operations as budget construction, fund raising, setting up bank accounts, and creating oversight of financial operations?

3. What resources must The New Ark require in order to survive as a church and to accomplish its goals?

4. If someone were willing to give this church a piece of property on which to erect a church building, would you recommend that it be accepted? Why?

5. What kind of building, should the members decide to build one, do you think would help accomplish this church's desired results?

See also the general questions listed on pages 28–29.

Symbol of New Ark Church

Two Approaches to Church Budgets

This appendix includes two actual local church budgets, each of which has a strength and each of which has a weakness. The first is the budget of a Presbyterian church in the central city of a large metropolitan area. It is a typical balance-sheet variety of budget providing comparisons to the previous year. Its strength is its detailed treatment of sources of income, a feature often missing in local church budgets. Its weakness is that there is no attempt to interpret how the expenses relate to the church's purpose or ministry. It is simply a balance sheet. It even tends to mask the fact that the church is facing an acute financial crisis.

By way of contrast, the second budget succeeds in interpreting the dollars to be spent in light of the intended purposes of the congregation, an urban church in a medium-sized city. This kind of interpretation is like that requested at the bottom of Table 14, Planning Sheet 1. As a result, the budget invites members to support the actual purposes of the church. The descriptions with the amounts change every year, so the educational benefit is cumulative. It also allows members to evaluate the church program. The second budget, however, fails to describe sources of income, and that constitutes its major weakness. Many budget items also lack comparisons with former years to show members how costs have risen or declined.

The first budget is for a congregation of 1,000 members, and the second congregation has 650 members.

A Downtown Presbyterian Church
1978 Budget

INCOME	1978	1977
Pledge contributions	$ 53,000	$ 50,000
Sunday loose offerings	1,400	1,400
Bequests & special gifts	10,000	12,500
Income from investments	17,700	17,700
Women's Association	500	500
Miscellaneous use of buildings	3,000	1,000
(Psychiatric center)	—	9,600
Music school & summer school	7,900	7,300
Manse apartments	3,000	3,095
Deacons' fund	800	800
One Great Hour of Sharing	1,000	1,000
Meals-on-Heels contributions	3,000	1,500
(Meals-on-Heels food income)	—	4,000
Rotary Club	3,830	3,750
Chinese congregation	400	400
Literacy volunteers	8,750	5,000
	$114,280	$119,545

EXPENSES	1978	1977
Administrative, Buildings & Grounds, Salaries		
Accountant's fee (part time)	$ 2,640	$ 2,520
Secretary, business manager	11,760	11,200
Sexton (plus apartment & utilities)	7,000	5,970
Assistant sexton (part time)	2,500	2,808
Typist (part time)	250	250
Fringe benefits		
Hospitalization (business manager, sexton)	770	685
Pension plan (business manager)	1,880	1,792
Payroll taxes	1,730	1,650
Church utilities	12,000	11,800
Church maintenance & repairs	5,400	7,000
Church garden	200	200
Manse utilities	5,000	4,400

Manse maintenance & repairs	1,000	1,400
Manse real estate & water taxes	730	730
Office supplies & machine maintenance	1,200	1,600
Postage	1,300	1,500
Printing	1,700	2,000
Telephone	3,000	3,000
Insurance	8,100	7,400
Audit fee	800	800
Miscellaneous	200	182
	$ 69,160	$ 68,887

COMMUNITY SERVICE

Assistant minister (plus apartment & utilities)	$ 2,640	$ 2,520
Hospitalization (one-half)	130	115
Payroll taxes	250	260
Cub Scouts, Brownies, Junior Girl Scouts (3 directors @ $270; Boy Scouts, $200)	1,010	1,010
Projection equipment & miscellaneous	70	67
Shared Meal, first Sunday	260	260
(Meals-on-Heels food cost)	—	4,000
	$ 4,360	$ 8,232

EDUCATION & SUNDAY-SCHOOL COMMITTEE

Seminarian (October through May)	$ 1,200	$ 1,200
Advertising & miscellaneous	600	750
Lenten ecumenical service	150	150
Religious education	700	700
	$ 2,650	$ 2,800

MUSIC & WORSHIP

Salaries		
Minister (plus apartment & utilities)	$ 13,125	$ 12,500
Choir director-organist	3,970	3,780
Director, primary choir	500	850
Fringe benefits		
Hospitalization (minister & choir director)	640	560

Travel allowance (minister)	500	750
Pension plan (minister)	2,640	2,496
Pension plan (organist)	635	605
Payroll taxes	1,350	1,280
Minister's discretionary fund	100	200
Soloists (36 weeks plus Lent)	3,700	3,700
Organ maintenance	200	200
Carillon maintenance	100	200
Piano tuning	60	80
Instrumentalists	800	800
Music & supplies	300	600
(Choir weekly coffee)	—	50
(Substitute organist, 5 weeks @ $40)	—	200
(Recognition dinner, choir)	—	200
(Annual visit of executive presbyter)	—	100
(Study leave expenses, minister)	—	400
	$ 28,620	$ 29,551

BENEVOLENCES

Mandatory

General Assembly	$ 490	$ 480
Synod	660	668
Presbytery	2,490	2,486
Ministerial salary supplement	510	506
Ministerial relief	100	105
Deacons' fund	800	800
One Great Hour of Sharing	1,000	1,000

Community council

Salary of Meals-on-Heels director, payroll taxes & overhead	3,000	2,720*
	$ 9,050	$ 8,765
Total Expenses	$113,840	$118,235
Income (or Deficit)	$ 440	–0–

*1977 Estimated overhead expenses for utilities, telephone, etc., for Meals-on-Heels $1,740; total Benevolences $10,505.

Program and Budget
1982
Otterbein Church

Mission and Benevolences

World Service Fund $24,770

This apportionment represents the basic mission obligation for United Methodist churches, divided as follows.

Ministerial support & education   9,165

This includes money for past pension funding for retired pastors, district superintendents' salaries, salary help for mission churches, and workmen's compensation for local churches.

Conference and denominational administration   3,220

World Service and Conference benevolences   12,385

This supports world and local missions, higher education, camping, retirement homes, hospitals, and Hispanic ministries.

One Great Hour of Sharing   2,400

This supports projects of the United Methodist Committee on Relief. If we surpass this goal, all money received is sent. All money given to this cause goes directly to meet project needs and not for administration. In the past 10 years our goal has increased from $300 to the present amount. The goal this year is $400 greater than last year.

Mission specials   2,200

This money helps persons in times of need, often following natural disaster. This past year, the Red Bird Mission High School (destroyed by fire) and Hospice were aided through these funds. These projects are usually supported through special offerings.

Mission advance specials   2,500

Churches that pay their World Service Fund obligation in full are encouraged to take on second-mile mission support. The following are projects we support.

Red Bird Mission, ministerial support   1,700

World Communion project   800

In 1981 this gave support to projects on the poverty-stricken island of La Gonâve in Haiti.

Pastors' discretionary fund   1,000

Supported by honorariums for pastoral services, this fund meets unexpected expenses such as meal and train tickets for transients and turning on heat for needy persons. It also meets nonbudgeted pastoral expenses.

Christmas gifts   200

Dr. and Mrs. (former pastor and wife)   100
Miss (retired missionary)   50
Rev. and Mrs. (missionaries)   50

Hospice of Lancaster   200

Hospice provides a ministry to individuals who are suffering from terminal illness and their families.

Radio broadcast   200

In March 1982, we will be broadcasting over WLAN.

Lancaster County Council of Churches   4,300

In addition to the items listed below, there is an "in kind" contribution of the clothing bank. We give this to the Christian Social Ministry at no charge. Our cash contribution supports the following.

Council programs   800

> These programs provide chaplains at Barnes Hall, local hospitals, and County Prison, and support Shared Holiday. This is an increase of $100.

Christian Social Ministry   2,500

> This provides funds for food, clothing, and furniture banks; Contact; migrant ministry; emergency aid; person-to-person ministry; and financial advisors. This is an increase of $100.

Food bank   500

> This offering is taken at our traditional Harvest Home service. This is an increase of $150.

Emergency funds for Christian Social Ministry   500

Clothing bank   3,000

This figure represents utilities and maintenance for the building provided by Otterbein Church.

Water Street Mission   100

This mission provides housing, meals, religious services, and jobs for transients.

American Bible Society   125

These funds help to provide scriptures at reasonable cost or free to blind, sight impaired, and persons of many languages. Literacy work through scriptures is also aided.

Manos House   150

Gate House (HEAR, Inc.)   150

These are local rehabilitation centers for drug addicts and alcoholics.

Fire and police   810

This is a contribution for these services so that city taxpayers do not have to pay an obligation that is rightfully ours. It amounts to 10% of what our tax bill would be if we were not tax exempt. This is an increase of $510.

Planned Parenthood of Lancaster   500

Family planning, physical exams, referrals to physicians and clinics, and education programs in schools are aided by our contribution. This is an increase of $100.

Ministerial student scholarship   1,000

This new item will show our tangible support to our ministerial student at United Theological Seminary.

Children and youth summer camping scholarships   1,200

We pay one-half the basic fee. In 1981, we had a record number attend. This is an increase of $300.

Mission capital funds   5,450

From 1981 to 1984, we are asked to contribute $21,800 to a capital funds drive to benefit camps, retirement homes, colleges, Methodist Hospital in Philadelphia, new mission churches, etc. These needs are urgent.

Miscellaneous   200

Total Missions and Benevolences $50,455

Christian Education and Fellowship

Education materials $4,300

This covers curriculum material and supplies for church school and other educational programs.

Honorariums	400

This includes guest preachers and teachers for worship and church school.

Church school picnic	325
Youth programs	900

Although our youth contribute significantly to their own projects, this helps fund a winter retreat, a spring retreat, and many other activities.

Teacher training	650

We depend upon the Parish Resource Center to provide many of the educational experiences for our teachers. The cost of membership is $225, and we pay registration fees for our teachers to attend special events. This year, during February, we have scheduled a special training event for all Otterbein teachers.

Softball	600

Most of this item is paid for by the softball team.

Kitchen supplies and food	4,000

Included in this is food for congregational dinners and other times of church fellowship, as well as the normal replacement of kitchen items. A new accounting procedure has been instituted in the kitchen with the hope that it will help us be better stewards.

Bus usage	1,000

For field trips, we have been able to save a significant amount of money by renting buses and providing our own drivers.

Total Christian Education and Fellowship	$12,175

Local Church Expense

Fuel	$10,000

Because of our new furnace and new conservation efforts, we have been able to hold the line on this item for the third year in a row.

Insurance	4,400

Every third year we rebid our insurance to ensure the lowest possible price. This will be done during 1982.

Electricity	2,600
Water	350
Janitorial supplies	650
Church maintenance	4,200
Capital improvements	4,300
Taxes (parking lot)	200
Office supplies	2,000
Printing	1,800

With the use of the new stencil-cutting machine, we have cut the outlay for printing substantially.

Postage	1,800

By distributing as much mail as possible on Sundays, we have been able to contain the cost of postage despite a 33% increase in first-class mailing costs.

Advertising	425
Church envelopes	400
Telephone	2,500

This includes the answering service with pager, which guarantees that a pastor can be reached at any time of the day or night; regular monthly service charge; and a significant number of long-distance calls when persons are hospitalized or have other personal needs outside the community. Between $300 and $400 of this figure is reimbursed by the Annual Conference for Conference business calls.

Music	1,900
Organ & piano maintenance	800
Christmas church decorations	200

Because we purchased our own decorations during 1980 and will now install them ourselves, we are able to realize a significant savings in this area. A significant cost that remains is for candles.

Pastors' travel	5,520
Flowers	550
Debt reduction	9,000

Our indebtedness, as of October 1, 1981, is $8,009. This money is owed to the Memorial Fund of Otterbein Church, and we do not pay interest on it. It is mandatory that we replace this money, and add to it, so that we can benefit from this type of interest-free loan from ourselves in the future.

Office equipment (capital expense)	2,000

Although it is not anticipated that we will need any office equipment during 1982, it was felt that this figure should remain in case of emergency.

Miscellaneous	1,300

One of the largest items in this category is the cost of deeds and perpetual care for cemetery lots that the church has for sale. The buyers pay these fees as part of the purchase price.

Total Local Church Expense	$56,895

Salary and Fringe Benefits

Rev. _____	$21,315
Rev. _____	20,515
Ministers' housing	9,785
Social Security	2,426
Ministers' pensions	5,503
Ministers' hospitalization	1,882
Director of music	4,235
Cherub Choir director	500
Organist	1,826
Substitute organist	200
Secretary	6,204

The secretary answers the phone and locates the pastors in the event of emergencies, in addition to caring for other office functions. Moreover, because of our location, the secretary deals with many drop-in persons who need help.

Financial steward	624
Custodian/sexton	8,107

Doesn't our church look great? In addition to keeping the church clean and inviting, the custodian/sexton opens the church for all meetings and makes sure it is closed when no one is here.

Custodian/sexton health insurance	689
Total Salary and Fringe Benefits	$83,811

1982 Total Budget

Missions and Benevolences	$ 50,455
Christian Education and Fellowship	12,175

Local Church Expense	56,895
Salary and Fringe Benefits	83,811
Total	$203,336

The increase in the budget from last year is $15,078, or an increase of 8%. It is projected that we will fall 8% short of our 1981 budget estimates. Therefore, this represents an increase of approximately 16% in real dollars.

APPENDIX III

Description of Community Types*

Midtown locale: the city's central business district, usually the location for banks, large department stores, and state or city office buildings.

Inner-city locale: generally one of the most deteriorating parts of the city. There is usually a high incidence of social problems, rundown housing, etc.

Inner-urban neighborhood: basically a residential area, but with some mixture of neighborhood-type businesses. Housing is generally two-family, middle income, or lower-middle income. This neighborhood tends to be an area of residence for ethnic groups or independent working persons' housing.

*Adapted from Douglas A. Walrath, "Social Change and Local Churches: 1951–1975" in *Understanding Church Growth and Decline: 1950–1978*, ed. Dean R. Hoge and David R. Roozen. (New York: The Pilgrim Press, 1979).

Outer-urban neighborhood: tends to be toward the edges of the city. Has middle-class to upper-middle-class housing, almost entirely single family, and few or no business establishments.

City suburbs: older, classic suburban communities that usually grew up along steam or electric transportation lines. They are aptly termed "sub-urb" because they grew as places of residence for commuters who were affluent and could afford to move out of the city. They still tend to be considered prestige residential locations and to have a community center and distinct community life.

Metropolitan suburbs: suburbs that have grown up as residential neighborhoods in a ring around the city. They tend to be arranged in a quiltlike pattern that intersperses residential locales, shopping centers, work locales, and entertainment centers, all connected by roads that ring the city. The basic transportation movement is around the ring, rather than in and out of the city. Travel is via private automobile rather than by any kind of public conveyance. The major development of these suburbs generally occurred after World War II.

Fringe suburbs: suburbs that have grown very recently, usually along interstate highway systems. They stand on the outskirts of the entire metropolitan area as city suburbs, in earlier times, grew up outside the city.

Fringe village: originally an independent rural village, but now overrun by the metropolitan area. Increasingly, housing has been purchased by younger middle-aged couples with children who are seeking a quiet village residence, but who in the rest of their lives are oriented toward the larger metropolitan area and world beyond the village. These communities tend to be a combination of long-term residents, many of whom are middle-aged or older, and these new arrivals.

Fringe settlements: former rural settlements that have recently been overrun by metropolitan expansion. Zoning is often poor, and land use is unplanned and irregular. Various types of housing appear including trailers, older houses, newer suburban-type homes, and a few estate-type residences. Some agricultural activity also remains in these areas. Most residents commute into the metropolitan area for employment.

Independent city: city that has not given rise to a metropolitan area but stands alone, generally dependent on one major industry. Many of these industries produce one product for which raw materials are close at hand—for example, cement or bricks. Both the industries and the cities that depend on them have been hard hit in recent years. Automation, synthetic substitutes, and foreign competition have all taken their toll. With reduced employment, these cities often suffer from urban blight. Only a fortunate few with an expanding industry (e.g., higher education) have not declined.

Rural village: the traditional business, commercial, and social hub of a surrounding agricultural area. With the decline of the number of people involved in agriculture over the last 20 years, however, many rural villages have either stayed the same size through out-migration of younger people or have actually declined in population.

Rural settlement: consists of a few houses, often a small church, sometimes one store or gas station, often now closed because of the competition of neighboring villages and the lack of travel through the settlements due to the bypassing interstate highway system.

APPENDIX IV

Data Collected from Sample Congregations

1. Full name of congregation
2. Address, telephone number
3. Date founded
4. Denominational affiliation
5. Pastors' names and addresses
6. Treasurer's name and address
7. Financial secretary's name and address
8. Manager of stewardship campaign, name and address
9. Manager of endowment, name and address
10. Community type (see Appendix III)

11. Census tract number
12. Membership: 1950, 1955, 1960, 1965–79
13. Worship attendance: 1950, 1955, 1960, 1965–79
14. Church-school attendance: 1950, 1955, 1960, 1965–79
15. Age distribution of membership (estimated)
16. Monthly receipts from offerings, 1977–79
17. Income in the following categories: 1950, 1955, 1960, 1965–79
    a. Offerings
    b. Gifts/bequests
    c. Endowment, trust funds
    d. Rental
    e. Fairs and bazaars
    f. Denominational subsidy
    g. All other income
18. Number of pledging units in categories from $1 to $100 or more a week
19. Information about accounting process
20. Spendable cash on hand, 1976–79
21. Information about nonprofessional staff and volunteers
    a. Number of persons paid in each category
    b. Hours per week paid
    c. Number of persons who volunteer in each category
    d. Hours per week volunteered
    e. Categories include:
       (1) secretary
       (2) organist
       (3) choir director
       (4) educational directors
       (5) teachers
       (6) soloists
       (7) janitor
       (8) sexton
       (9) business manager
       (10) community service personnel
       (11) other

22. Worth of endowment: 1950, 1955, 1960, 1965–79
23. Restrictions on use of endowment
24. Uses to which income from endowment has been put
25. History of major maintenance of property
26. Description of property owned by congregation
27. Expenditure data: 1950, 1955, 1965–79
    a. pastoral services
    b. debt reduction
    c. utilities
        (1) fuel oil
        (2) gas
        (3) electricity
        (4) snow removal
        (5) water
        (6) telephone
        (7) other
    d. insurance costs
    e. all nonprofessional staff costs
    f. music program costs
    g. benevolence (local)
    h. benevolence (denominational)
    i. educational program costs
    j. maintenance costs
    k. supplies cost
    l. total expenditure
28. Details about each loan negotiated by the congregation
29. Description of fund-raising procedures
30. Dates of service of present and former pastors
31. Opinions of church financial leaders (see Chapter IV)

SELECTED BIBLIOGRAPHY

Preliminary Reports of the Economics of American Protestant Congregations Project

Hartley, Loyde H. *Economics of American Protestant Congregations, Preliminary Report*. Hartford, CT: Hartford Seminary Foundation, 1980.

———. "Inflation and Recession Hit the Local Church Budgets," in *Yearbook of American and Canadian Churches, 1981*, Constant H. Jacquet, ed. Nashville: Abingdon Press, 1981.

———. "Inflation Hits the Congregational Budget," *JSAC Grapevine*, Vol. 12, No. 1. Joint Action and Strategy Committee, 475 Riverside Drive, New York, June 1980.

Long, Stephen H. *The Economics of American Protestant Congregations*. Hartford, CT: Hartford Seminary Foundation, 1978.

Ecclesiology

Brunner, Emil. *The Misunderstanding of the Church*. London: Lutterworth Press, 1952.

Gustafson, James M. *Treasure in Earthen Vessels*. New York: Harper & Row, 1961.

Jones, James W. *Filled with New Wine*. New York: Harper & Row, 1974.

Küng, Hans. *The Church*. New York: Sheed & Ward, 1967.

MacGregor, Geddes. *Corpus Christi*. Philadelphia: Westminster Press, 1958.

Moltmann, Jürgen. *The Church in the Power of the Spirit*. New York: Harper & Row, 1975.

Niebuhr, H. Richard. *Christ and Culture*. New York: Harper & Row, 1951.

————. *The Purpose of the Church and Its Ministry*. New York: Harper & Row, 1956.

Paul, Robert S. *The Church in Search of Itself*. Grand Rapids: Eerdmans, 1972.

Welch, Claude. *The Reality of the Church*. New York: Charles Scribner's Sons, 1958.

Economic Trends for Religious Groups

American Association of Fund-Raising Counsel, Inc. *Giving U.S.A.* New York. Annual.

Commission on Private Philanthropy and Public Needs, John H. Filer, chair. *Giving in America: Toward a Stronger Voluntary Sector*. Washington, 1975.

Commission on Stewardship, National Council of Churches. *Church Financial Statistics and Related Data*. New York. Annual.

Jacquet, Constant H., ed. *Yearbook of American and Canadian Churches*. Nashville: Abingdon Press. Annual.

Johnson, Douglas W., and George W. Cornell. *Punctured Preconceptions: What North American Christians Think About the Church*. New York: Friendship Press, 1972.

Systems Perspectives on Local Church Economic Issues

Azzi, Corry, and Ronald Ehrenberg. "Household Allocation of Time and Church Attendance." *Journal of Political Economy* 83 (1974): 27–56.

Blank, Frederic, and Robert Shelton. "An Economic Analysis of
Religious Mergers." Mimeographed. Department of Eco-
nomics, University of Wyoming, Laramie, WY, n.d.
Leach, William H. "Financing the Local Church." *Annals of the
American Academy of Political and Social Science* 332
(November 1960): 70–79.
Long, Stephen H. "Financing Voluntary Organizations: A Test of
the Social Pressure Hypothesis," in *The Voluntary Nonprofit
Sector*, Burton A. Weisbrod, ed. Lexington, MA: Lexington
Books, 1977.
————, and Russell F. Settle. "Household Allocation of Time and
Church Attendance: Some Additional Evidence." *Journal of
Political Economy* 85 (1977): 409–13.
Weisbrod, Burton A., and Stephen H. Long, ed. "Concepts and
Measures," in Burton A. Weisbrod, *The Size of the Voluntary
Nonprofit Sector*. Madison: Institute for Research on Poverty,
University of Wisconsin, 1977.

Theological Perspectives on Church Finances

Anderson, Michael D. *A Present Witness*. Wilton, CT: Morehouse-
Barlow, 1975.
Brattgard, Helge. *God's Stewards: A Theological Study of the Prin-
ciples of Stewardship*. Minneapolis: Augsburg, 1963.
Briggs, Edwin A., ed. *Theological Perspectives of Stewardship*.
Evanston, IL: General Board of the Laity of the United
Methodist Church, 1967.
Brueggemann, Walter. *The Land: Place as Gift, Promise and Chal-
lenge in Biblical Faith*. Philadelphia: Fortress Press, 1977.
Carlson, Martin E. *Why People Give*. New York: National Council
of Churches, 1968.
Dietze, Charles. *God's Trustees*. St. Louis: Bethany Press, 1976.
Dulles, Avery. *A Church to Believe In*. New York: Crossroad Pub-
lishing Co., 1982.
Hengel, Martin. *Property and Riches in the Early Church*.
Philadelphia: Fortress Press, 1974.
Kantonen, T.A., *A Theology for Christian Stewardship*. Philadel-
phia: Fortress Press, 1956.

Piper, Otto A. *The Christian Meaning of Money*. Englewood Cliffs, NJ: Prentice-Hall, 1965.

Salstrand, George A.E. *The Story of Stewardship in the United States of America*. Grand Rapids, MI: Baker Book House, 1956.

Savage, Dennis B. *One Life to Spend*. St. Louis: Bethany Press, 1962.

Stone, Glen C., et al. *A New Ethic for a New Church*. New York: Friendship Press, 1971.

Towards a Christian Attitude to Money: Papers and Findings from an Ecumenical Consultation. Geneva: World Council of Churches, 1966.

Ecological Perspectives on Religion and Finance

Byron, William. *Toward Stewardship: An Interim Ethic of Poverty, Power and Pollution*. Paramus, NJ: Paulist/Newman Press, 1975.

Cauthen, Kenneth. *The Ethics of Enjoyment*. Atlanta, GA: John Knox Press, 1975.

Elder, Frederick. *Crisis in Eden: A Religious Study of Man and Environment*. Nashville: Abingdon Press, 1970.

Heiss, Richard L., and Noel F. McInnis, eds. *Can Man Care for the Earth?* Nashville: Abingdon Press, 1971.

Keech, William J. *The Life I Owe*. Valley Forge, PA: Judson Press, 1963.

Mooneyham, W. Stanley. *What Do You Say to a Hungry World?* Waco, TX: Word Inc., 1975.

Shriver, Donald W. *Rich Man, Poor Man*. Atlanta, GA: John Knox Press, 1961.

Taylor, Richard K. *Economics and the Gospel.* New York: United Church Press, 1973.

Ward, Barbara, and Rene Dubos. *Only One Earth*. New York: W.W. Norton & Co., 1972.

Financial Management Procedures for Local Churches

Cashman, Robert. *The Finances of a Church*. New York: Harper & Row, 1949.

Energy Efficiency: An Energy Management Program for Churches and Synagogues. Washington: Edison Electric Institute, 1983.

Holck, Manfred Jr., *Accounting Methods for the Small Church.* Minneapolis: Augsburg, 1961.

———. *Money and Your Church.* New Canaan, CT: Keats Publishing, 1974.

———, and Holck, Manfred Sr. *Complete Handbook of Church Accounting.* Englewood Cliffs, NJ: Prentice-Hall, 1978.

Janzen, Lester E. *The Central Church Treasury.* Newton, KS: Faith and Life Press, 1968.

Johnson, F. Earnest, and J. Emory Ackerman. *The Church as Employer, Money Raiser, and Investor.* New York: Harper & Row, 1959.

Peterson, Robert E. *Handling the Church's Money.* St. Louis: Bethany Press, 1965.

Total Environmental Action, Inc. *The Energy-efficient Church: How to Save Energy (and money) in Your Church,* ed. Douglas R. Hoffman. New York: The Pilgrim Press, 1979.

Stewardship and Fund Raising for the Local Churches

Journal of Stewardship. New York: Commission on Stewardship, National Council of the Churches of Christ in the United States of America, 1979.

Knudsen, Raymond B. *New Models for Financing the Local Church.* New York: Association Press, 1974.

MacNaughton, John H. *Stewardship: Method and Myth.* New York: Seabury Press, 1975.

Murphy, Nordan C. *Commitment Plan Handbook.* New York: National Council of Churches, 1973.

Pendleton, Othniel A. Jr. *New Techniques for Church Fund Raising.* New York: McGraw-Hill, 1955.

Rieke, Thomas C., and John C. Espie. *Opportunities in Stewardship.* Nashville: Discipleship Resources, 1975.

Representative Nineteenth-century Works on Church Finances

Dodds, John. *Christian Beneficence.* Dayton, OH: United Brethren Publishing House, 1896.

Harbaugh, H. *A Plea for the Lord's Portion of a Christian's Wealth; in Life by Gift, at Death by Will*. Daniel Miller, 1885.

Stall, Sylvanus. *How to Pay Church Debts and How to Keep Churches out of Debt*. New York: I.K. Funk & Co., 1880.

Some Special Problems in Church Finances

Balk, Alfred. *The Religion Business*. Atlanta, GA: John Knox Press, 1968.

Berger, Hilbert J. *Time to Negotiate: Guidelines for Pastors to Follow When Salary Support Is Considered*. New York: Friendship Press, 1973.

Hartley, Loyde H. *A Study of Clergy Support in Pennsylvania Southeast Conference, The United Church of Christ*. Research Center in Religion and Society, Lancaster, PA, 1972.

Kelley, Dean M. *Why Churches Should Not Pay Taxes*. New York: Harper & Row, 1977.

Larson, Martin A., and C. Stanley Lowell. *The Religious Empire*. Washington: Robert B. Luce Co., 1976.

Leas, Speed B., and Paul L. Kittlaus. *Church Fights: Managing Conflict in the Local Church*. Philadelphia: Westminster Press, 1973.

Lewis, G. Douglas. *Resolving Church Conflict: A Case Study Approach for Local Churches*. New York: Harper & Row, 1981.

Robertson, D.B. *Should Churches Be Taxed?* Philadelphia: Westminster Press, 1968.

Stiles, Joseph. *Acquiring and Developing Church Real Estate*. Englewood Cliffs, NJ: Prentice-Hall, 1965.

INDEX